Explaining Things

Explaining Things

Inventing Ourselves and Our Worlds

Lee Thayer

Author of *Communication!;*
Doing Life; and others

Library of Congress Control Number: 2010919177
ISBN: Hardcover   978-1-4568-4040-2
                 Softcover   978-1-4568-4039-6
                 Ebook   978-1-4568-4041-9

This book was printed in the United States of America.

To order additional copies of this book, contact:
Xlibris Corporation
1-888-795-4274
www.Xlibris.com
Orders@Xlibris.com
82732

For KT, whose explanations, inspirations, and aspirations make life so richly rewarding.

CONTENTS

APOLOGIA

Everyone who has ever written about the human condition is limning all of those who have previously written about the human condition. Not *all*, actually. Only those he has read. Even then, he limns only those whose work he admired, or otherwise found compatible with his own.

This is all a very unconscious process. When we speak or write, we do so from our own minds, not the minds of others.

Academicians (I passed through there) are by convention interested in the lineage of the ideas they entertain. They use attributions to convince others that their ideas are inevitable in the tree of knowledge they are swinging from. They attribute support for their own ideas from the idea-celebrities of the past and present. Attribution is invariably strategic.

No one—scholars included—could actually sort out his or her own ideas from those they have imbibed in their own mental pasts. Ideas give birth to ideas. No mind is innocent. We put our own spin on what we take in.

The end result is an amalgam. The original is often lost in the spinning out of ideas that struck a chord in someone's mind.

To challenge the maxim that it is always too late for the truth, I here present my ideas as my own, which is what they are. That they owe *everything* to all of the ideas that I have taken in from others, but have interpreted to suit my own, is a given.

Ideas are cheap. It is what is made of them that matters in life, and in society. So here are some ideas—unadorned—for you to consider and decide what you can make of them.

I have done my homework. Take my word for it. I have been imbibing the best ideas I could find about the topics addressed in the following pages for sixty-five years. If I don't call out particular sources, it is because there have been hundreds—nay, thousands—of them. So many they would impede your reading.

And that would be counter-productive. Jump in and struggle. I did.

Lee Thayer
November, 2010

INTRODUCTION

*"The way a question is asked limits and
disposes the ways in which any answer
right or wrong may be given.*

Susanne Langer

How do we want to pose the question here so that the answers it provokes can be both useful and practical?

I think the question we want to ask here is this:

**How could we understand our compulsion for always
explaining things so that we understand ourselves
better, and so we can conduct our lives in ways
that enrich us rather than continue to diminish us?**

In other words, how can we explain ourselves and our world in a way that raises us up rather than puts us down?

The error of our ways is assuming that when we are explaining things, we are uncovering reality. There is not much reason to believe that this is the case. True, we have remarkable and ever-more-powerful technologies in our lives. But these did not come from explaining *them*. They came from the raw desire on the part of a very few to accomplish something beyond what was presently possible.

It was the famous and innovative physicist Michael Faraday who invented the electric motor. He was one of the greatest experimental scientists in history.

He concluded—of seminal importance to us here—that *human perception is not a direct consequence of any "reality," but is rather an act of imagination.*

What Faraday the *physicist* is saying is that all so-called "reality" is mediated by the human mind. We have no direct contact with reality. This is the same point made by Einstein when he said that we have to have theories in order to catch "facts," that any facts we claim are the products of the human-invented theories we bring to bear.

This is a great launching pad for the question we have raised. But first we need a more pragmatic perspective on why this compulsion to explain things is so inescapable for we humans.

We live in the *virtual worlds* of our minds. Our minds mediate *everything.* Humans may have some sort of contact with some sort of reality before they learn how to talk. But that would be a mindless existence, from our point of view—totally naïve.

It is in interacting with other humans—verbally or nonverbally—that our minds get created and maintained. We become *somebody*—a particular *person*—initially because others tell us who we are. Thus begin the lifelong endeavors of consciousness and self-consciousness.

We learn the *meanings* of things in our environment by observing what those things seem to mean to those around us. The people around us inevitably change. When they change, what things and people mean to us change with the people we talk to most often.

Our minds are always a work in progress. Our minds are a product of the communication which swirls around us all of our lives. Every mind is infected by the minds of those with whom we fall into communication, whether directly or indirectly (for example, with the media).

Who would be talking about "love" or about "human rights" if they had never heard of those subjects?

The worlds people create when they talk about them are *virtual worlds,* created and maintained by **how** they talk about those virtual worlds.

LEE THAYER

What we believe depends upon those people around us who ratify those beliefs.

In any human society of any size—from two to thousands or even millions—people's minds get more or less synchronized. By and large, we see approximately what others see, we feel approximately what others feel, we believe what others believe, and we think what others think.

This synchronization is never perfect, of course. If it were, we would have no need to communicate. As we say, even though we abuse and misuse them, we like to think we have our own individual minds. Everyone does. But not one exists independently of the other minds that infect it.

The point of this minor digression is as follows:

> *In the last century, our "scientists" (e.g., our so-called social "scientists") decided that since minds could not be studied*
> *like cells because they could not be dissected, they were not worth studying. So they threw out the term and went for the corporeal brain. Now we are told that we do what we do because our brains tell us so.*
> *Impossible.*
> *Those same "scientists" do what they do because they communicate with one another.*
> *What they do is apparently **meaningful** to them—a condition that would be impossible if they lived in the world they say they live in.*
> *Human meanings are a product of human minds. The universe is meaningful only to the humans who say it is. What something means depends upon what we humans say it means. Nothing has meaning in and of itself.*

And, finally, it just doesn't make any sense to talk about "explaining things" apart from the people who do it and the *minds* they do it with.

It has been observed in many cultures over the history of humankind that

> **Explaining things** *is at the very core of human mental activity. It can be considered what defines us as human.*

We may not best be described as Homo sapiens, but as Homo *explanans*—the creature who explains himself to himself, and who explains all the rest of the world in ways consistent with that explanation. We are the creatures who are apparently *compelled* to explain everything. This is especially the case—maybe uniquely the case—in the Western episteme. We create a culture to live in, and then our culture creates us to fit.

We have to explain things. That's what people do. If you are not constantly explaining things, you have not yet matured in Western civilization.

We inevitably created a culture to live in simply because it is in talking to one another that we create that culture. Any human culture is an ongoing product of how its members have explained things. For example, every marriage has its own culture. The two people create that culture, and then it creates them. Every tribe, every clan, every civilization has evolved in the same way.

Janet Frame is the New Zealand writer (*Living in Maniototo*) who describes our times as

> "*The Age of Explanation, an era in which articulate people have almost explained themselves away.*"

That is, if you can talk, you are a co-conspirator. The more we explain, the more we have to explain. Evolution itself may be a bit hokey. But explaining things is not. It is like a cancer, over us, below us, around us.

We cause the cancer. And then it causes us.

We are bored because we have run out of people to explain ourselves to. We are bored because our lives are stunted by all of the understanding we have to suffer as a consequence of our incessant explaining. Then we have to explain *that* situation.

Freud was right. We create our own personal heavens and hells by how we explain them.

We are restless because we are "truth-seekers." The American Indian (and other civilizations) were "truth-keepers." Their bottom-line truth was *beauty*.

The Navajo, for example, began life with their truths. All that was left for subsequent generations was to do whatever they did "in beauty." These are remarkably different ways of living on earth.

We more "modern" Westerners, by contrast, think of our own lives and the life of our civilization as being *linear*. For the American Indian, as for the Polynesians and others, their lives and their societies were *cyclical*. They always returned to where they started. Time was a "puddle," not a matter of "progress."

These considerations are not just interesting. They are indispensable. You can't get the most advantageous handle on "explaining things" without these considerations.

Our own culture is not a natural thing. It got incubated over many years by many different people. It is a product of people—of how people over time have explained things to each other. So it cannot be taken as a given. Previous cultures were not wrong. They only look wrong—"primitive"—from our point of view.

If cultures are made by people talking to one another—explaining things to each other—and then our cultures make us, we need to learn how to explain things in a way that raises us up, not puts us down.

That is why this book exists. There are better ways of explaining things—to our own great advantage as humans. This book provides a sort of foundation for learning how to explain things in a more humane way.

A demeaning culture leads to desperate people. That is surely not what we dream of for ourselves and our children.

> "... the notion that verbal behavior can be other than explanatory is a vanity of vanities."
> —Pierre Janet (1928)

We can add to that all kinds of dress, comportment, possessions, and every other form of so-called nonverbal behavior. Anything that a person can take into account communicatively is a form of explanation. Such understandings *explain* who we are, both to ourselves and to others.

To speak is to explain. Humans have no choice but to explain *everything* to themselves—via the minds they have for doing so. Any utterance already assumes processing by someone's mind. It is all interpretation (or translation). It all adds up to the virtual world in which each of us lives, and in which we all live collectively.

How we talk to ourselves, and *how* others talk to us (directly or indirectly) provides us with a "self." We become who we *are* in the process. And we remain who we are by explaining ourselves in the same kinds of ways, and by others' interpretations of us.

Put us in a radically different culture, and we cease to be who we were and become someone else as required by that new culture. Spouses who get remarried have to learn the rules all over again in that new and different culture. If they don't, they will have serious problems.

So, if one is identified by oneself and others, his way of explaining things (including himself) have to remain fairly consistent.

One way of looking at this is that every explanation proffered and ratified by others is a trap. It may be an unavoidable trap. But it is still a trap. We have to stay on the path premised by our explanations, or we will have trouble with others. We may want to change. But if that change is troublesome to others, it would have to be *approved* by those others.

In the way of previewing the sometimes counter-intuitive concepts that are set forth in this book, we can consider yet another fundamental perspective. It is that

> *"Humanity itself was created in narration."*

What this can be taken to mean is that both consciousness and self-consciousness get formed in the *stories* we tell. They are the major vehicle for explaining ourselves to ourselves and to others.

Stories are enchanting. Listen to people gossiping today. We can get engaged in a movie or a TV drama. We can become a part of the action. We can identify with the characters. We take away the lessons for living that we are capable of taking away. It is how we learn to become the kinds of humans acceptable to the cultures in which we happen to live.

We internalize stories. We do not internalize the calculus or an ideology that does not interest us. Abstract ideas do not affect us much, unless they are our own. Stories that serve our appetite for stories are compelling. Great writers are alchemists. They seduce their readers or their audiences according to susceptibilities of those particular readers or audiences, just as lovers do.

We are victims of the stories we have imported—or the stories that compel us at the moment.

And, as we shall see in greater detail in this book, *all explanations are stories*. They tell a story (at least implicitly) that satisfies our appetites of the moment, whether amusing, suggestive, or angering.

It is easy to consume the stories that most appeal to us at the moment. But many people consume the wrong ones.

There are some immensely useful practical aspects of all this business of explaining things.

For example, the columnist and quipster Evan Esar shared some old folklore:

> *"The less you know about a subject, the longer it takes*
> *you to explain it."*

That's not totally true, of course. But that's the way it seems. You can test out that theory on yourself. There are certain aspects of explaining things that seem proverbial. The more thoroughly we understand the basic human proclivity for explaining things, the better we understand people.

There is much more of the like up ahead in this book.

Laurence Stallings wrote the screenplay for *She Wore a Yellow Ribbon*. He gave John Wayne this line:

> *"Never apologize and never explain—it's a sign of weakness."*

It can certainly be construed by others that way. Your friends will understand your explanations anyway. And your critics will not believe you anyway. Here I am paraphrasing Elbert Hubbard, one of the great homespun American philosophers.

All in all, the subject of explaining things is a many-splendored thing, which itself calls for explaining in all it richness. It is the process by which we invent ourselves and our human societies. We have to know what we can about the process in order to avoid being victimized, and in order to avoid being an unintentional accessory to the crimes that are committed in the name of merely explaining things.

We cannot participate in the social world without explaining things. We cannot avoid having things explained to us in ways that may not be in our best interests.

Yet we can learn how to do so more critically.

That is why *this* cautionary tale exists.

1

Explaining Things Invents Us

When Willie Sutton, the least psychologically corrupted of bank robbers, was asked why he robbed banks, he replied, "Because that is where the money is."

Most people think of explaining things as a harmless, even neutral activity. It is so much more than that . . . if we really knew.

People explain themselves—as Willie Sutton did above. People explain the world we all live in—sometimes to our detriment. We expect people to explain any behavior that falls outside the norms, or the social mores.

People don't tell us what we need to know. They tell us what *they* happen to know—which tells us more about them than it does what they are talking about. If people are asked, they don't answer "Yes" or "No." They more typically launch into a lecture or a story we didn't ask for.

We bring many explanations from our past as baggage. We live 24/7 in a world of swirling explanations—from commentaries on television to the burgeoning so-called social media. Everyone wants to explain things to us. And we feel compelled to return the torture.

That's the obvious, superficial part of it. What is not so obvious is how we get invented as sentient human beings in the explanatory soup we exist in.

When you were a babe, everything in your world was explained to you. As you got older, you became an explainer as well as an explained-to. When you were being explained-to, your mind was being formed and constructed. When you became an explainer, you used your mind as it was formed at that moment to explain things to others.

Explanations you understood (or believed) became the original structure of your particular mind, casting a long shadow across your future. When you became capable of explaining things to yourself, you questioned some of those early explanations and began to create explanations of your own—to test out in the real world.

We are literally built up from the explanations we have been—and continue to be—exposed to. We are continuously becoming who we are by the explanations we buy into and those we proffer.

Communication is more than just exchanges of information. We are usually busy explaining our take on things (or telling a story, which amounts to the same thing), or being exposed to someone else's stories or explanations. Whether we are explaining or being explained-to, who we *are* is continuously being formed and reformed.

Tribes of all sizes—from a friendship or marriage to a civilization—are also constantly being formed and reformed in accordance with their members' explanations of things.

So the ultimate consequence of how we explain things is who we become, and the destinies of the larger cultures we all inhabit. This is dynamic. It never ceases. In some irreducible and inscrutable way, we become how we explain things—both individually and collectively.

Questions and Answers

If you ask a question, you are not just asking for information. You are explaining to others who you are.

If you answer a question, you are not just providing an answer, you are at the same time explaining to anyone who is curious just who you are.

This stems from the fact that you cannot speak without revealing who you are. And you cannot field others' utterances without revealing who you are by how you do so. We are continuously becoming who we *are*.

You cannot engage in communication with others—or with any of the media—without being affected in some small or large way.

We evolve individually and collectively in our patterns of communication, and in the implications of what we are exposed to there. What engages us is our minds. And our minds are always a work in progress.

We cannot engage other minds either directly or indirectly without implicitly explaining who we are and what we're up to. A novelist explains his story. An artist explains her conception of what she paints. A scientist explains himself by what he says and does, a friend no less.

We assume we want to know what is going on in the world today, so that is the question that tunes us in. The journalist answers our question by telling us what he or she knows. Neighbors and friends converge via *gossip*—which is telling and being told. We explain to each other who we are by how we explain things and by how we field others' explanations.

Underneath the superficial activities—of the games people play communicatively—there is always this process of making and being made in explanations. We become who we are individually and collectively by how we explain things and by how we are explained-to.

A relationship is formed by a question and its answer. The other wants to know who you *are* by a direct or a hidden question. We tell the other who we are by how we answer.

Explaining and being-explained-to are the building blocks of all human social life. What become social mores was once just a question. Our mores—our customs—are our collective answer to that question.

A question you can't ask is an aspect of who you *might have become* if you had been able to ask it.

An answer is always looking for a question to attach itself to. An explanation is always looking for a situation to exercise itself in. People become relevant by asking the questions for which others have the answer, and having at the ready answers for the questions others might ask. The limelight is always on the explainer. Being the star for even a minute or two may explain why people put themselves into situations where they have to *explain* themselves.

In the myriad ways we engage in explaining things, it is arguably the most inescapable mechanism of human and social life. We live and die by our explanations. It is exciting to explain why we love another, or why we love something. It is devastating when someone explains they don't love us.

Explanations have brought us to where we are. Explanations will define our destiny, and take us there.

Where there is human life, it will be *explained*. And as it is explained, so will we humans *be*. *We invent ourselves in our explanations, and then our explanations invent us.*

Meaning

We are stuck from the outset with this need to explain things.

That's because the primary tool we use to navigate the world is our minds. And our minds deal only in *meanings*. Minds are not very good at dealing with the raw material of the world—natural or social.

It is our minds that mediate our existence. And they deal almost exclusively in the *meanings of things*—to us. Thus we have to know not only that there are happenings and people and ideas and images in the world we inhabit. We have to know what all of those things mean before we can deal with them.

Our minds thus provide us with a kind of *virtual* reality. There is a reality out there beyond us and beyond our control, for certain. But there are only a handful of people equipped to play with that reality. Even then, if they want to talk about it or explain it, they have to use words and other human metaphors—like theories or other such explanations.

A small elite may claim to be scientific. But when they want to talk about their speculations, they have to do so in the *virtual worlds* of what things mean—to them and to the others they want to explain things to.

The world of meanings is created and maintained by humans—in communication with one another.

We become human and join in the fun and the agony only when we are meaningful to ourselves and to others.

We create meanings out of the meanings that exist or have existed. Old meanings do not die. They just get transformed into new ones.

To explain something to ourselves or to others is a game. What's at stake are meanings. Either they accept the meanings we proffer, or we acquiesce to their meanings. Or, we could collaboratively create new meanings that suit us both in some minimal way. Love is like that.

It's a social game every human has to learn how to play—or is simply excluded. It doesn't seem very gamey because it seems so natural. But it has inescapable consequences. We can never know exactly what those will be. And we usually don't give it much thought, even if we could know. We just play along.

Life is made up of meanings. So we just play along, on the assumption that it's just the way it is.

Actually, that assumption is well-founded. We may have secret meanings. But if we want to be a part of society, we have to realize that meanings are ultimately social, not personal.

If you want to have conversation with people, you have to have rough idea of what meanings they will attach to what you say. A satisfactory conversation by two or more minds requires that they can translate sympathetically—two or more minds that are reasonably similar in their workings. They have to be speaking the same language, which involves ways of expressing things, and ways of understanding what is expressed.

People speak. But what they *mean* by what they say *has to be* provided by the recipient(s). You can imagine you know what you mean by what you say. But nothing in the natural or the social world arrives with its meaning on its back. That always and inevitably has to be provided by the humans involved.

If the other(s) do not understand what you mean by what you say, they may ask you to explain what you mean.

As the humor columnist Evan Esar put it,

> *"When a politician makes an explanation, the explanation has to be explained."*

Not just politicians. All communication in which we engage is also political—in some degree.

Since people can only guess what we mean by what we say, we can lie, deceive, dissemble, and win by rhetoric or maneuver. Self-interests and hidden agendas are always involved. All communication is political in this sense. So are all explanations. Who knows what we are trying to achieve with our explanations? Others can only guess what we *mean* by what we say. Sometimes even we do not know what we mean by what we say.

We are trying to maneuver in someone else's virtual world (their minds) by using our own virtual world. When it comes to understanding, we can only understand what all that means, using our own minds.

We *have to* communicate in these virtual worlds. We can claim all the truth and all the facts we want to. They still have to be translated—made meaningful—by others. In the end, it is of no great consequence what *we* mean by what *we* say or do—except insofar as that aids us in explaining ourselves to others.

Everything—certainly all of the consequences—are given in how others attach *meaning* to what we say or do. (Or what we don't say, or don't do.) It is others' minds that can always trump us.

If what we say or do is not transparent to others, we may be called upon to explain ourselves.

It is not the explanation as such that matters. It is the meaning that others impose upon that explanation. Every explanation has to be interpreted by the person(s) who are involved.

We want what we say and what we do to be appropriately interpreted by others. Whenever that is *not* the case—which is frequently—we may be called upon to explain. Certain explanations will be accepted in certain relationships and in certain cultures. Others won't.

If you don't know the rules of explaining things—whether in a marriage or in statesmanship—you lose the game.

> **We become what we can explain.**
> **What we can't explain we cannot *be*.**

Explaining Things to Oneself

The preeminent determinates in all explanations are the people involved. It is they who decide.

The world is not obligated to be the way we explain it. In much the same way, no person is *obligated* to accept or to proffer any explanation. Everything hinges on how he or she explains things to themselves. This always precedes how they explain things to others, as well as what might be acceptable as an explanation to those others.

Any and all explanation has a precondition. It is how people explain things to themselves—before, during, or after the explanation.

You could explain in great detail why it is in this other person's interest to reciprocate the love you profess. But if that person has no interest in you, it will be for naught. Marketers can wax eloquent about the advantages of their product. But if there are people at whom this is directed who cannot imagine explaining to themselves why they would buy your product—they probably won't.

The Israelis can explain that they mean well. But if this is not imaginable in how those in the West Bank explain things to themselves, then it makes no difference whether or not the Israelis mean well.

People will be persuaded. But they will most often be persuaded by how they explain things to themselves and not by how someone explains something in a contrary way.

The point here is that facts and arguments are compelling only to those people who are susceptible because of the way they explain things to themselves.

No "truth" will not compel a person who has a contrary point of view. Reality will win over people who live in a different reality—a contrary way of explaining things.

To be rational is usually an entreaty to think like we do. To be irrational is to fail to agree with or be persuaded by us. So both rationality and irrationality are customs shared by people who explain things in much the same way.

There are some people you can understand quite well until they begin to explain themselves. How people explain things to themselves is always private and inaccessible to others. There is always therefore a private world which is unseen by you—and is neither controllable nor subject to direct manipulation by you. You have to guess what you're up against.

In Lewis Carroll's *Alice's Adventures in Wonderland* (1865), Alice is given to say,

> "*I can't explain* myself, *I'm afraid, sir,*" *said Alice,* "*because I'm not myself, you see.*"
> "*I don't see,*" *said the Caterpillar.*

What makes Carroll's work so endearing and lasting is that it is much more like everyday life than are the conventions of many of our other stories. There is much in everyday life that doesn't make any sense. But we *make it* make sense to us and move on. So we don't see much of the absurdity of our ways.

We *assume* that Alice *is* herself if she is explaining herself. Otherwise we would be in "wonderland" ourselves. So like the Caterpillar, we "can't see," because who people believe themselves to be is something we have no access to.

If a person explains herself, we have to assume that she is who she is—unless you're a psychiatrist, in which case you *consciously* play your games in wonderland.

How most people explain things to themselves is constantly changing. Are they no more and no less than how they explain things to themselves? If a spouse explains to herself that she doesn't love you any more, is she *herself*? Or is she just not herself from your point of view?

In an 1813 letter to Thomas Jefferson, John Adams wrote:

> *"You and I ought not to die before we have explained ourselves to each other."*

Why would he say that? And at what point in their lives should they do this explaining of themselves to each other?

Because our minds are abuzz with inputting and outputting every day, we literally spend our lives trying to explain who we are. This has its root in explaining ourselves to ourselves. But it involves everyone and everything we are in communication with. We may change our minds about all of this usually in some small way. But how we explain things to ourselves will always precede, accompany, or open the door to later rationalizations of how others try to explain things to us.

So how Adams tasked Jefferson is for most people a perennial chore. To explain yourself to others requires you first to explain yourself to yourself. Most people can't do this.

> *We live in two worlds simultaneously. We live in the world of our own minds. But as we grow out of infancy, we also live in the world of other minds. There is always a struggle. How others explain things is the primary constraint on the prerogative we imagine we have to do our own explaining.*

How we accommodate others' explanations will always be a function of how we would explain the same thing. How others would accommodate our explanations of things will always be a function of how they would explain the same thing.

The *struggle* is that between synchronization and de-synchronization. What isn't accommodated jeopardizes the social order. What is accommodated reinforces it. The social order may be something as small as a personal relationship or as large as disagreements between or among nations.

It is certainly possible that the war on America as declared by bin Laden is an attempt to slow or preclude the "Westernization" of the Muslim way of life. If that were the case, would the so-called terrorism be justified?

"Understanding"

All of this obviously has a lot to do with what different people understand and how they do so. The example in microcosm here may again be marriage, or any other close, ongoing relationship.

We may understand another person because it is our desire to do so. That doesn't mean we *really* understand the other person, or that the other person *really* understands herself. "Falling in love"—which is a form of mild insanity—requires each person to abandon the need to explain oneself to oneself in favor of letting the other person do this for them. After all, people fall in love with someone who thinks more highly of them than they do of themselves. They safely assume during the honeymoon that each is trading up. They view themselves much more positively than they did before the *falling* occurred.

The problem arises when the other person begins explaining us more negatively than we would. When one or the other begins to understand the other in a critical rather than an uplifting light, trouble begins.

It is the same with nations, with ethnic groups, with factions of any sort. It is just easier to see when using the microcosm as an example.

When people want to understand in some mutual way, things go reasonably well. When they begin to misunderstand a previously shared understanding, things turn south.

> *To explain things is minimally an invitation to negotiate a mutual understanding of those things.*

Understandings are never neutral. They have all sorts of consequences—both for the one who understands and for the larger civilization.

It may seem perverse, but *understanding* is both a door-opener and a door-closer. We progress by our understandings of things. But in what direction? To what ends?

Understanding has its advantages. But it is also a kind of *trap*. To understand someone else is usually interpreted by that someone else as agreement. We can thus synchronize our minds. But understanding carries no warranty, even implied. Are we understanding what we *should be* understanding? Lovers and allies who *need* each other understand each other.

But when one no longer *needs* the other, what happens to their mutual understanding?

A person may "understand," but will that get him or us where he or we ought to be going? An understanding may run contrary to what we want or what we ought to do or be. What then? The *trap* has already sprung.

All understandings have this paradoxical nature. We can do things with it. But it can do things to us that may not be in our own best self-interests—because our explanations invent us.

Understandings do not have to undergo a morality test, even if we could make one.

We understand—we *believe*—for all kinds of reasons. None of those beliefs guarantee that the resulting understanding will lead us where we want to go, or ought to go.

Sir James Hopwood Jeans, the eminent British astrophysicist and questioner, wrote the following in his 1942 book *Physics and Philosophy*. For anyone who wants to think about explaining things, it bears pondering:

> *"Physics tries to discover the pattern of events which controls the phenomena we observe. But we can never know what this pattern means or how it originates; and even if some superior intelligence were to tell us, we should find the explanation unintelligible."*

That may be a roundabout way of saying that we can only understand what we can understand, or that we can only explain things in a way that we can understand. If so, it is worth pondering the dilemma.

If someone explained how something actually happened, we might not understand it. In a light-hearted way, there is something of this in Willie Sutton's explanation of why he robbed banks. What did the interrogator want him to say?

> It is at least possible that what we can't understand is
> more important than what we can understand. But that
> would be difficult to explain, since we are entrapped in
> what we can understand.

The Era of "Expertise"

A strange thing happened on our way to the 20th-21st centuries.

For many generations, people knew what they needed to do to farm, to raise animals, to run a small business, to travel, to provide homemade remedies for various illnesses, to handle their own finances, etc. That has changed, and it is a major change in our culture.

My own grandparents were self-sufficient. They could do everything they needed to do to perpetuate their lives and the farm. My Irish grandfather, for example, could make harnesses for the horses, and could repair his old hay rake annually with the tools and materials at hand. Birth and death were family affairs. I was born in the same bed as was my mother, attended by my grandmother and a neighbor.

That was only two generations ago, early in the 20th century. We no longer know how to do things for ourselves. We are chattel to our "experts." This has put us all in a very vulnerable and even untenable condition.

True, the world we try to live in has become complex beyond our comprehension. There used to be only a handful of roles to be mastered for life. Now there are thousands, and they proliferate daily. Our freedoms and our control over nature have come at a great cost. We live securely these days in a pharmaceutical hothouse.

The witty columnist Evan Esar, whom we have encountered before, penned the following:

> *"The reputation of an expert is sometimes based on what he knows, but more often on what others don't know."*

It is the latter part of that comment that compels our attention here. We have to be *ignorant* of more and more circumstances that bear upon our modern lives in order to create the need for *experts* of every stripe.

Experts are thus social predators. We are their willing—or at least complicit—prey. In this great cultural sea-change, we want our doctors to manage our health and illness, our financial advisors to manage our money, and our educational experts to manage our learning in our years of involuntary servitude in our schools. We want our culinary experts to tell us how and what to cook, our celebrities to tell us how to live, our political experts to tell us how they are going to save us.

We want our plumbers to tell us why the faucet is leaking, our professional farming experts to tell us what to plant and when and where, our pastors to explain to us what the Bible says.

There are people who never raise their blinds to look outside. They depend upon the radio weather report to know what's happening on the other side of the window. They have to be told that they may want to carry an umbrella, or to slow down when driving in a snow storm.

We seem to relish the dependency because we are inclined to increase that dependency every day. All we have to do is be more ignorant than we were yesterday about how to make and maintain our lives. That seems to suit the modern ethos.

What does all this have to do with how we get invented as persons and as civilizations in the process of explaining things?

It has everything to do with it. We used to be participants in inventing ourselves and our cultures. We are now in the bleachers. We will depend upon the experts to tell us what is going on—and what it means to us. To go from playing the game to watching the game be played and explained *to us* is a momentous change in human cultures generally.

As Evan Esar put it,

> *"Some men do things, while others just sit around and become experts on how things should be done."*

The experts are not always right. They are often just *wrong*. In his recent book with the lengthy subtitle—*Wrong: Why Experts Keep Failing Us—and How to Know When Not to Trust Them*—David Freedman compiles the facts on the experts. For example, "90 percent of physicians' medical knowledge has been found to be substantially or completely wrong."

When people managed their own health and illness, their lives were at stake. Experts live at arm's length: it is not their lives that are at risk, only the mistakes that they bury. Your trusted financial advisor will either be lucky or just plain *wrong*. Experts will always have an explanation for whatever happened.

But of course we all do.

Culturally, what is happening is that the world we have to live in is increasingly being mediated by various experts. Whether scientists or hucksters, the world we *see* is concocted and disseminated by them.

The experts have done us much good. We live longer, we have more creature comforts, we can go anywhere with our Blackberries and our cameras, and are secure from many diseases that used to ravage us.

But there is something very pernicious about their ascendance as the mediators of our life on earth. All experts belong to an alien culture. They have to have crossed-over. As they mediate more and more of our world, we begin to belong to their culture and not to our own.

These days, if you ask a person what she thinks about something, she will likely tell you what she's picked up from the experts. More and more, those experts do our thinking for us so we don't have to. There is even some evidence that our brains actually shut down in the onslaught of expert advice about everything under the sun.

We are no longer the protagonists in making ourselves in our own image, however haphazard and arbitrary that may have been. The experts are taking over—with our complicity of course. We are increasingly living in *their* culture, not the one we inherited from our predecessors.

If this is the case, then we will become the way(s) the experts explain us.

This may turn out to be better for us. But when the control over our destinies goes over to an alien culture, we had better be wary and skeptical. *Because they are usually wrong, just as we are.*

If we are wrong, there's a possibility *we* could make it right. If *they* are wrong, we have to depend upon them to make it right—and there is little reason to believe that they know how to do that.

So Who "Are" We?

We are not born knowing how to think and feel and act in a human-made world. We have no choice but to be made—constructed—to suit that particular human-made world we are born into. Our parents saw to that. Then other people do.

Our conscious minds are created and maintained primarily in communication with our compeers, employing whatever media are available.

We *mind* the world in ways that are approximately how the people in our culture and subcultures do. We can relate to them and they to us only to the extent we do so. We "mind" ourselves—we see and relate to ourselves—according to the mind we have for doing so. We are *people* because we think and feel and act like people in our culture think and feel and act.

In that sense, we invent *ourselves*. We do so usually not intentionally, but inadvertently and inescapably.

We become who we *are* by how we explain ourselves, how we explain the world we live in, and how we explain one another. That prerogative may be usurped, as our look at the "experts" revealed. But becoming a reasonably acceptable human being requires our complicity, no matter the forces at play. We learned how to be serfs of the manor, and we forgot how to be lords of the manor. All social machinery is reciprocal.

So who *are* we now?

We are some combination of how we explain ourselves and of how we get explained by others, either directly or implicitly. It is never wholly our call.

We are a product of all of the explanations we have been exposed to, whether others' or our own.

We are built out of those explanations. If we think they are not important, then that explanation makes us unimportant to ourselves and to others.

Our relevance to ourselves and to the world of people in which we live will be decided by how we explain things. We may be wrong. But we can never escape our own complicity in the process by which we get invented and become who we will become.

Once we utter or understand an explanation, we are no longer innocent. The legend of the "fall" was the fall from innocence.

2

Humans, the Explainers

*"To arrive at the concept of the quark by
mathematics, and to believe that this is an
objective, scientific, truthful explanation of
what's at the heart of all matter, that it explains
something about the universe, is as fabulous
a demonstration of story-telling as anything that
mankind—scientific or otherwise—has ever
pulled off."*

—John Jerome, in *Stone Work* (1989)

To be a practicing human being requires being a fabulist—a person who explains things, and who makes up a story to give credence to his or her explanations.

It is rooted in the Western episteme that we are compelled to explain. We are compelled to explain ourselves at any moment. We are compelled to explain the universe. We are compelled to explain our lives and the societies in which we live. And we are compelled to explain our explanations.

Every explanation needs a context. That is the *story* that frames and is intended to justify our explanations. We explore the universe. We wouldn't have to. But the story in which our feverish need to explain the universe provides the necessity for doing so—if you believe the story. We explain why we did what we did. We concoct a plausible *story* to justify why we did what we did.

We lead ourselves this way. And others lead us by their explanations and by the stories they tell to justify their explanations. We invent the explanations and the stories. And then *they* invent *us* (to paraphrase Winston Churchill).

We have no choice. Ours is a truth-*seeking* culture. All of our truths are provisional. They are only good until a better truth comes along. We are like Sisyphus. We are condemned to push our truth-stones to the top of the hill, only to have them roll back and we must repeat the process again and again.

What we can't explain is why we became a truth-*seeking* rather than a truth-*keeping* kind of culture. Our story is that those were primitive cultures, and that the people were ignorant. We don't want to be ignorant. We want to explain *everything*.

Even love fades away when the lover knows everything there is to know about the other. What we seek is lost in the compulsion to seek on and on forever.

Love does not stay. Why would it? We have to *explain* it. Some things have to be experienced, not explained.

But a cultural compulsion is a compulsion. We can't let anything stand in our way. Everything must be *explained*.

"Tells"

How do we "read" others? How do they read us? How do we unveil the hidden premises from what is being said and done? How do we deduce the explainer from the explanation?

"Tells" is a term well known to champion poker players. It refers to the subtle facial and body language clues they use to decipher what their opponents' strategies are likely to be, and the hands they are holding. They win more often, they say, because they are so good at reading "tells" after years of experience.

When we explain ourselves, we tell people who we are. When we explain other people or something going on in the world, we tell people who we are. When we act or don't act, we tell people who we are. It is impossible *not* to provide such implicit details to anyone who is capable of *reading* them.

And others will do so. It is impossible to speak without being judged. It is impossible to refrain from speaking and not be judged. People are always looking underneath our overt speech or actions to assess who we are. It is usually not our intention. But they will do so anyway.

So our explanations are not just about what we might be talking about. They also reveal who we are.

> We are who we are because we explain things the way we do. The explanations we proffer and the explanations we internalize are, taken together, who we are.

The best poker players work hard at *not* providing tells to their opponents. But even that can be a "tell." There is no possible way of avoiding being read by others. They are compelled to explain us, with no obligatory regard for our intentions in the matter.

We are always complicit (even if involuntarily) in their reading of us. And they are always complicit in the strategies by which we attempt to evade their reading of us.

Tells reveal us to those who can and wish to read them.

We always implicitly reveal who we are by how we explain things—or avoid explaining things.

People *read* us whether we are aware of it or not. They may read us wrong. Either way—right or wrong—their readings become a part of the social world we have to adapt to. If we don't, they will marginalize us.

Tells are never simple. A cunning player may perform a "tell" in order to throw his opponents off track. In other words, players can lie, they can deceive. If the superior player does not pick up on this, he or she loses.

It is the same in social life. People rarely perform who they *are*. In their roles of the moment, they perform what others might think they are. They experiment. They might perform as they would like to be seen. They may not care. But all social life is thus mutually-strategic in nature.

People cannot avoid trying to explain to themselves who you are. This is what makes it possible for you to lie, or to deceive. They are only guessing from the way you perform yourself. Perform yourself differently and they will concoct a different conception of you.

In the end, however, it is those other people who have the prerogative of accepting or rejecting, of believing or disbelieving who you seem to be—given your performance. You might influence them if you are a compelling performer and provide them with the "tells" that support your intentions. But it is still their call. You may affect their call. But who you are at the end of the game or the end of life is never totally your call.

As Abraham Lincoln was said to have said,

> *"You can fool some of the people some of the time,*
> *but you cannot fool all of the people all of the time."*

A "tell" is a small unconscious or unintentional bit of behavior that you may not be aware of. But others can look at it as a way of *explaining* to themselves who you are and what you're up to.

The process of explaining things is going on all of the time, whether people are aware of it or not.

Because other people pick up on the "tells" they believe to be relevant to *their* purposes, all human lives are to that degree inadvertent. What we intend may not be read by others that way. What we don't intend can be read anyway, and sometimes to our disadvantage.

It is the person who knows how to strategize his own tells and who knows how to read others' tells who has the most control over his own life. And the most influence on others' lives.

"Resistance" to Change

There is talk. And then there is behavior. The two are not tied together of necessity.

Most people can talk a good story about change. But when it comes right down to it, it's mostly talk. Most people do not change much over their adult lives. If you want to know what a person is going to be like tomorrow, your best hypothesis is that he or she will be much the same as they were today.

When seriously ill and dying people were told by their doctors that they would die soon if they didn't change their ways—their lifestyles—what do you suppose happened? *95% of them couldn't change even though their own lives were at risk.*

What *were* they thinking?

The doctors' pronouncements were rational. Much of human behavior is not. So the pronouncements and the subsequent behavior belonged to two different worlds—two quite different logics.

These patients may have wanted to die just to escape the badness of their lives. But there is a simple and far more empirical reason for what happened. It can be generalized to the need for change and the so-called resistance to change across the board.

It is that who you are at any point in your life is an indeterminate amalgam of all of the ways in which you have explained things—and been explained to—over the course of your life. What's at stake is changing who you are or simply staying on as who you are.

It is in this sense your *identity*—who you are to yourself that is at risk in any significant change. The scales will always tip on the side of who you *have* been, not how you *might* be or even hope to be.

People often have hopes and dreams. But the forces of the past will likely keep them who they were, and not who they might wish to be. They can't become who they would need to be in order to *live* their dreams.

The cliché is that we want to marry the man or woman "of our dreams." The reason that seldom happens past the honeymoon is that the person merely having the dream is not capable of being the person she or he would need to be to *live* that dream—to make that dream come true.

How we *have* explained things is almost always a more powerful force than how we would *need* to explain things to be someone else.

Change does occur. But it is usually independent of our wishes. We know how to wish upon a star. But we typically haven't got what it takes to explain things from the perspective of the wish realized.

We usually don't proactively resist change. It's just that how we have explained things (and ourselves) for years is so much a part of who we are that we just can't make the leap.

The Social Order

All human societies and all human endeavors are ordered in some way. One especially fruitful tack to take here is that all societies, gatherings, organizations, etc. are ordered along the lines of *who can explain what to whom.*

Explanations are not just a way of telling or being told. They organize the social, commercial, political, aesthetic, and legal worlds in which we live. At the same time, they create the comprehension behind the comprehensible worlds we inhabit with our minds, our feelings, and our actions.

You may try. But you do not *tell* the cop who pulls you over for speeding. He tells you. When you are a child, you do not tell your parents what's what. They tell you. When you are an adolescent, they do not any longer tell you what's what. You begin to tell them, at least in our modern Western cultures. You do not *tell* the teacher. She tells you. You can try to tell your doctor (in 18 seconds) how you feel. But in the end, he or she is the one to tell you what's wrong and what to do about it.

You do not tell the retail clerk or the customer service person what's what. In a subtle but certain way, they tell you. The grocery store tells you how to eat by what it has to offer. You cannot coerce a person into falling in love with you. He or she tells *you* what's possible.

You do not tell a Senator or the President or a celebrity. They tell you. You do not tell your computer what you want it to do. It tells you what's possible, given how it is programmed. In the air, the lowly flight attendant tells you what you can and cannot do.

You can propose something to God. But God disposes. The commandment requires that you be thankful for whatever He dishes out to you.

Who can explain what to whom is the mechanism behind the pecking order—behind status. Hierarchy is ubiquitous in nature. It is ubiquitous in all cultures that are not yet "modern." We moderns would like to believe that we would be better off with some other arrangement. But no human organization, from marriage to the federal government, will work except hierarchically. It's been tried.

That's because of this underlying prerequisite. If someone doesn't have the prerogative to explain things to others, it becomes a social quagmire. Even a primitive hunting party cannot function as a whole unless someone can explain what to do to the others.

There is no coherent collective without this underlying mechanism of *who gets to explain what to whom.* It's been tried in modern marriage. But modern marriages-by-choice do not last as long or as harmoniously as arranged ones. We moderns seem to prefer our egalitarianism over efficacy. We believe the principle is more important than the consequences.

There will always be a social order. But it is difficult to see how the process of everyone talking to everyone about everything is going to lead to a happy ending.

We can change the people in a hierarchy if it isn't working as it should. But we cannot change the people in a free-for-all when it is their *right* to do and say as they wish at any moment. Their prerogatives are more precious to them than the consequences.

You can rail at oppression. But you can also do something about it. You can rail at rights over responsibilities. But you can't do anything about that. Unimpaired freedoms become their own prisons, as any thoughtful adolescent will tell you. Their suicide rate is appalling.

If we don't know where social order comes from, we can't fix it. We could fix the underlying condition. Knowing that it is *who can explain what to whom* might help.

An Explanation Is a Generalization

One of the problems created by our incessant and compulsive need to explain things is that our explanations are often taken as exemplars. They become useful as a *category* of explanations. Used over and over again, they become clichés, which people can use without really thinking about them.

For example, a person may tell anyone who will listen the stories of his life—over and over again. After awhile, there is no certainty that the stories he tells actually happened. Once people come to believe those stories, they become rote. They are repeated over and over again just because the teller is so familiar with them—not because they are in any sense true.

So we create and fixate ourselves—and create and fixate the images others have of us—by offering up our clichéd stories.

Similar ways of explaining things by many people over a period of time becomes the framework of their culture. All the rest is complementary décor. To emphasize once again: *First we create our culture by how we explain things. Then our culture creates us and our progeny.*

Most ways of explaining things that catch on are generalized to explain successive situations that look the same. We look at the world through the prisms of our explanations of it. It is our explanations that create our immediate reality. Our lives take the shape and the directions that our explanations implicitly point to.

In general.

What's in a Name?

The German-born American physician and wit Martin H. Fischer made this observation in the 1940's:

"When there is no explanation, they give it a name, which immediately explains everything."

What he is suggesting is that we cluster our understandings and our images of people or events around the name given to a person or an event or an object. We use the name to conjure up the multi-faceted concept we have of that person, event, or object.

How we *conceive* of something is indexed by the name which is given to it.

For example, we name babies. We use the baby's name to call up our memories about, our intentions toward, and our images of that child. After a while, we understand our *concept* of the child, not the child herself. We give names to our feelings so we can call them up and perform them. We often give pet names to those with whom we are in daily contact. It's a kind of shorthand for opening the door to a trove of memories and expectations.

Scientists give a name to what it is they want to talk about. That makes it real. It offers a public hook on which to hang a lot of theories and other explanations.

Physicians don't know what to do until they have named our malady. The name gives the malady we experience only by how we talk about it. Since medical science can treat only what is made "objective" by naming it, now it can be diagnosed and treated.

We try to explain what's going on subjectively. But it isn't until it is called by its abstract name that it becomes objective. The name offers a way of moving on.

What doesn't have a name is incomprehensible. The key to what *is* comprehensible is how we have named it—how the name conjures up our image and understandings of it.

What we do in the name of love depends entirely on how we individually define or *explain* the private concept thus named. Love has as many meanings as it has explanations and enactments.

What's in a name is all of the meanings a person can associate with that name. We are *explaining things* when we give anything a name.

Explanations Are Illusions

No explanation is ever the same thing as what is being explained. We live in the illusory worlds of our explanations. It's all the so-called reality we have. It is easy for us to operate *as* if those explanations were our reality.

The name we give to people or events is not the same thing as those people or events. We merely and casually assume that they are.

There is *nothing* until people *explain* those aspects of the world they want to talk about. What we say about things is never the same as those things. The word elephant is not the same thing as the creature. The *word* Mary is not the same thing as the person we are calling Mary. A quark (the word) is not what the physicist assumes he is observing.

It is merely the name for what he assumes he is observing.

Our minds do not—can not—observe the phenomena of the world. They can only deal with the concepts we impose upon things when we explain them—what things *mean* to us. We do not live in any objective *reality*. We live in the world of illusions we have created by how we explain things. Our realities exist in what we say things *mean* to us.

In *The Myth of Sisyphus*, Albert Camus wrote:

> "*A world that can be explained even with bad reasons
> is a familiar world. But in a universe suddenly divested
> of illusions and light, man feels an alien, a stranger.*"

What this famous writer is trying to tell us in his literary work is that we *need* our illusions. When there emerged minds in the modern world that wanted to make our world and all the people in it **literal**, we began to feel like aliens in our own world. We are strangers in a strange land. We are not the kind of creatures who can live literally. We need the illusions that are created and maintained every day in how we explain things.

Those explanations may be wrong. But it is in them that we humans must live.

Any attempt to destroy our illusions destroys our humanity. We have to live not in the things of the world, but in the *meaning* of those things to us.

Scientism would claim *reality* as its exclusive domain. It seeks the literal "truth" of things. This is a form of explaining things, becoming hegemonic, that would reduce us to wholly-determined robots. For example, we would be reduced to brain functions not controlled by us, or reduced to our genetic heritage.

All Ways of Explaining Things Have Consequences

What this should alert us to is this:

> *Just because it is necessary for us to explain everything*
> *doesn't mean that we are going to get it right.*
> *Some ways of explaining things may be good for us.*
> *But some may be bad for us.*
> *And the only judge we can ask is . . . us.*

Any way of explaining things has consequences. It has consequences for the explainer, and it has consequences for the culture.

For the explainer, it makes public what otherwise could remain his or her secretive life. What we explain in private has no more claim on us than we give it, reluctantly or otherwise. What we explain in public has a certain claim on us. Others hold us accountable. Thus we become accountable for our explanations.

How we explain things individually influences how we *can* explain things going forward.

How large numbers of people explain things collectively not only closes out other possibilities. It colors or discolors the culture going forward.

The tragedy is that we don't know and don't care. We assume we don't have to suffer the consequences. We are alive and adapted or maladapted to the lives we have at the moment. We have little interest in history going forward—even our influence on it or its influence on us.

But there are always consequences. We may not be aware of them. We may not care. But the present is always a product of the past. We don't know how we got to be the way we are. We don't care—as long as we have another day or year ahead of us.

We don't even want to think about what nasty impositions we lay on our progeny. We are happier when short-sighted. Let the future take care of itself. There will always be mothers and politicians to do this for us.

We are reluctant to take our explanations seriously. They take us seriously. They will make us or future generations pay the price for our indifference.

For we moderns, *freedom* is the freedom to do what we want and say what we want. These are the very activities that need to be most constrained.

The German poet Goethe said that we must love people not for what they are, but for what they could be—what they *should* be. If we applied that to ourselves, we should approve of ourselves only if we are on the path to becoming what we *should* become as humans.

But we don't seem to know or care know what path we should be going down. We have no long-range purpose for our own lives. We have no image of what our culture should be like in order to provide us with the richest context for humanizing ourselves.

We just go along, explaining ourselves and our worlds with little thought given to where this is going to lead us.

We may be the creatures that *have to* explain things. But that didn't come with a guarantee that how we do so would be good for us.

So the crunch questions may be:

> *How would you explain yourself if you intended to be a better human being tomorrow than you were today? Would you then explain yourself differently?*

*How would you explain things if you wanted
your explanations to* enhance *the cultural
world you inhabit?*

Past civilizations were different from ours. We may say they were primitive, and that ours is far advanced. But those are words of our own making. No primitive person ever explained himself or herself as being primitive.

The American Indians had a saying. It was along these lines:

*"Before you speak, be certain that what you are about
to say is going to add to the beauty that already exists
in the world."*

To them, the natural world was sacred *because* it was so beautiful (to them). To them, their fellow-travelers in this world were also sacred.

We use and abuse the natural world. Now it is ugly. In the same way, we use and abuse our fellow-travelers. We dehumanize them if it suits us. That's what demographics are all about. What we learn in our civilization is how to manipulate others for our own purposes.

We got here by how our forebears explained things—things like science and technology. In our rush to progress, we lost what it meant to be content with what we have. American Indians presumably had few communicable diseases until the Europeans arrived on the scene. We snuffed those cultures out because of the way we explained them. They were savages, to be treated as the inferiors we explained them to be.

What we did to these mostly gentle civilizations we are capable of doing to ourselves—by how we *explain things*. The "savages" of the far Pacific worked an hour or so a day. Given our work-days, it's not so obvious that they were ignorant people belonging to backward cultures.

In our explanations of ourselves, all else in our world, and where we ought to be going, we may not have got it right.

We could rethink how we explain things if we considered it might be all that important.

Which it is.

3

Why We Explain *Everything*

> *". . . if you want to have fun, make up explanations. Give people reasons if they want reasons. Anything you want. Make reasons up. It'll surprise you—the more improbable the reasons, the more satisfied people will be."*
>
> —David Foster Wallace, in
> *Girl with Curious Hair* (1989)

There are five basic reasons for why we explain things:

1. We personally feel compelled to explain ourselves to ourselves or to others.
2. They say or we believe that others *expect us* to explain ourselves.
3. We have to explain whatever people want to pay attention to or want to talk about.
4. We just like to hear ourselves talk about what we *can* explain.
5. Exponentially so, there are those folk whose role in society is and who get paid for "reporting"—or otherwise explaining events and worlds to which the rest of us have no direct access.

It would be useful to look at each of these in some depth.

Explaining Ourselves to Ourselves and to Others

Humans are stuck with creating an explanation for things that are either incomprehensible or ambiguous. People—like the events of the natural world—are both.

We make up a way of comprehending them in general. In particular, it is never quite so easy. When in contact with others, we start with a small understanding and build forever (if possible) on that. Infants open up to caring parents and other adults. They keep their distance if they are uncertain about the outcome.

Adults are more likely to use stereotypes and prejudices. These possibilities exist only for youngsters and adults who have learned how to use them as shortcuts. Most often, we don't really want to *know* the other person. All we need is a barely-adequate understanding of the other that enables us to move on in a conversation or a relationship.

Lovers don't really *know* each other or even what "love" is supposed to mean—to them. But that hasn't stopped anyone yet.

At the outset, we try to *explain* ourselves to each other, in various ways. In the process, we recreate ourselves along the lines of the image the other has of us.

A person who interviews for a job at your place tries to explain himself by putting a spin on things he thinks others will respond to favorably. When he meets and greets his fellow employees, he is spinning all the time. But then, so are they. Getting into a relationship requires a lot of accommodation on both sides.

So who we are is always some amalgam of who we imagine we are and what others imagine we are. No one is autonomous *in* any human group or society. We always get created and recreated in *some* cultural context. We can play at creating ourselves only so far as permitted by how others see us, or want us to be.

We can privately explain ourselves to ourselves. But if our performance of who we imagine we are doesn't get accepted by the others around us, we are essentially grounded until we get it right in *their* eyes.

So explaining oneself to others is a very sophisticated process of sanctions. We can endorse ourselves. But we can't be the person we imagine ourselves to be until we have been sanctioned by those around us. Leaders, for example, are never self-made, in spite of the proclivity to believe so. They have to be endorsed as their leader by others.

Celebrities have to be endorsed by their fans. Who gets to be the teacher has to be endorsed by those who are going to play the game. It is the same with who gets to be "the boss." Or who gets to be "the expert." Or who gets to be "the lover." Or the one who gets to explain.

There are writers and there are readers. But they can be neither one until they mutually endorse one another.

People explain themselves by how they play the roles they happen to be—or choose to be—in. Other people have expectations. If those are not met, your explanation of yourself may amount to nothing.

Explaining yourself to others—whatever form it takes—and explaining yourself to yourself are forever in some kind of precarious balance. A politician who is a hero today may be a goat tomorrow in the eyes of her constituency. But many politicians succeed by being whoever their constituents desire or expect them to be.

So do friends and lovers and teammates and celebrities.

When a spouse or a subordinate do not perform as desired or expected, there is trouble. But, then, that may be what was desired or expected.

Maslow's much-heralded fantasy of "self-actualization" is misleading on at least two counts. One is that very few people are ever straining to self-actualize themselves. The other is that if the auditors in your circles of friends and acquaintances don't want you to actualize yourself (whatever that may mean to you or them), it just can't happen unless you get a whole different set of auditors.

Who you are or who you can be is always a matter of reciprocation. If I need you to change, I can't change. And conversely. Changing together requires starting over. And that ranges from extremely difficult to impossible.

When you try to explain yourself to others (whatever the form that takes), you are not performing to a blank slate. Because the other has interests and needs and a history of his own, it will be imperfect—at best.

So where do you start when you want to explain yourself to yourself? Do you begin with an ideal? Or do you begin with what you have read, what you have heard, what you have experienced, or with your own personal and private fantasies?

How you explain yourself to yourself will always be constrained by how others expect you to explain yourself to *them*. Your fantasies are not *their* fantasies.

If you want to be a part of a human group or society, you *have to* be a strategic negotiator. If you can't do that superbly, your voice won't amount to much.

Becoming *someone* requires the endorsement of others, unless you want to play it the way Emily Dickinson did. She took the risk of being irrelevant to society in order to achieve the sheer acquiescence of others to her fantasies. Most people don't have the financial or the personal resources to do that.

So most people simply take the ways in which others explain them as their own. They explain themselves to themselves quite like others explain them.

If you wanted to be someone other than who others imagine you to be, you would either have to become a highly persuasive explainer. Or you would have to find that group or circle that would endorse you. There is no third option.

When Others Expect or Demand

There are social norms and mores about acceptable speech and behavior. If what you said or did fall outside these rules, you may be called upon to explain yourself.

Sometimes what you say or do may not be readily comprehensible to others. In this case, you may again be called upon to explain what you said or did.

A third possibility occurs when others can't figure out what you *meant* by what you said or did. They would not be asking you to offer your meaning for what you said or did. They would be asking you to offer an acceptable meaning to *them*.

The process of socialization is that of inculcating in you what's proper and what isn't, what's meaningful to others (and what isn't), and how your *conscience* is supposed to work in public. What we call social change is what happens when people are not perfectly socialized.

Doing your own thing may be okay in private. But there are always limits and boundaries when others are present.

You may feel free to dish your mother or your boss among your friends, but not when your mother or your boss are present.

So how we behave or talk depends upon whose company we are in. Chameleon-like, we adapt to the norms of the people whose company we are in.

What's intriguing here is this:

> The more diverse the cultures we want to move in, the more codes of conduct we have to learn. We almost never present ourselves. We present a self that is acceptable. Our lives are chock full of deceit and dissembling—of posturing and politicking. We see it as a necessity until it becomes a habit. Then we no longer question the lies we tell ourselves and others.

Any explanation we offer to justify or redeem ourselves is more often than not what we would call a necessary deceit. Sometimes small, sometimes not. We get to be so good at this that we no longer know who we really are. We are just ways of explaining ourselves and presenting ourselves according to what other people have come to expect of us. We just sort of change colors depending upon who is present.

There has been much talk in recent years about being authentic. This comes at a time when people are increasingly inauthentic—that is, when they comport themselves as they intuit might be called for given the circumstances.

> We play whatever social game is being played.

The critical challenge to any serious thinking here is simply this:

If being authentic means being candidly open in what we say and do, then the idea is doomed from the outset. The "truth" would be anathema to most human relationships or any human society.

Interaction between and among people is built on illusion and metaphor. When people talk to themselves (which is most of the time), they have an image of themselves which is *inescapably* illusory.

We use human-made words and images. These are therefore once removed from any reality. In use, they become *our* reality—a *virtual reality* made of words and images produced and consumed by people. A name or other explanation produces a concept. And we see the world in and through the lenses of our concepts of it.

Humans *have to* live in the virtual worlds produced by how things have been explained.

How things are explained—and our minds are congeries of explanations—is always illusory, in the sense that an explanation is itself never the thing being explained. A culture is a conglomeration of the most used and useful explanations of things.

The illusions we live in and live by are not in any way signs of mental illness. They are simply necessary for making minds and making and sustaining human societies with those minds.

The Necessity to Explain Things

Whatever we humans want to understand—or are compelled to understand—has to be explained.

People explain the world to us. We explain the world to ourselves. If we want to understand something together, we have to explain it. It might be a person, a happening, or some visual or auditory aspect of our environments. It might be an idea, or a concept like love or freedom. To talk about things in any way requires transforming them from reality and giving them virtual reality in how we talk about them.

The 20th-century Romanian-born French playwright Eugene Ionesco wrote (in 1969):

> *"Explanation separates us from astonishment, which is the only gateway to the incomprehensible."*

Although Ionesco is exercising his unique prerogative as a playwright, there are ways of thinking about explaining things here that are worth exploring.

First, there is this distinction between what is comprehensible and what is not. We comprehend what we explain. But we also explain what is, to us, incomprehensible. What we don't comprehend, we explain by way of myth or fairy tale, a hired mystic, or even one or another of our human religions.

We have ghosts and fairy tales to explain certain happenings that are otherwise incomprehensible. We have science to explain the workings of the world we cannot see. We have UFOs to explain certain space aliens. We have soothsayers, palm and tea readers, and we have financial advisors. These and many more can explain the inexplicable—e.g., what the stock market is going to do, or what the future holds for you.

There are more astrologers in the U.S. than there are astronomers. One tells you what your future holds.

There are those who call up the spirits of the dead. There are others who claim to predict such natural phenomena as the end of life on earth.

Just about as much money is spent on crystal-ball gazers, Tarot cards, and bean-throws as on getting an education.

People want to know what is unknowable. They will pay for this, even though the payee is making up the explanation. We will pay dearly for converting the incomprehensible into the comprehensible. People don't believe this, but you are more likely to be struck by lightning than you are to win the lottery.

Second, it is as if people compulsively need to avoid being astonished. So they put the explanation between them and the incomprehensible. Over the years, people have *believed* the strangest things. It is a satisfactory explanation that comforts us, never any bedrock truth.

We are discomfited by the truth. We prefer an untruth that we like. A famous artist once said "We have art to protect us from reality." Art—like science, technology, rhetoric, and other forms of *explaining things*—are human creations that separate us from reality.

Inventors, like Thomas Edison, are not trying to reveal and bring us closer to nature. They are building a world that shields us from nature—just as philosophy does.

We can live with false prophets. We can't live with randomness. So we eliminate it from our lives as best we can. As David Wallace says at the top of this chapter, what we can't understand we make up an explanation for. We live in our explanations, which make comprehensible what would otherwise be incomprehensible.

You cannot experience other people's experiences. People can only explain them. Being stymied by this, some modern pseudo-scientists would have you believe that the *mind* is explained by explaining the brain. They can't locate the mind tangibly, so they take something tangible to explain what is incomprehensible to them. Metaphors abound. The *mind* was at one time considered to be just a more complex computer.

There are people who still believe that. They are the same people who believe that the brain can explain everyday human behavior.

Ionesco is saying that we are *all* fabulists, not just playwrights or writers of fiction.

Explanation and Mental "Diarrhea"

That's a metaphor, of course. But when people talk on and on, explaining what they happen to know, it might be an apt one.

It would be no exaggeration to say that people *love* to tell other people what they happen to know today. It may be irrelevant to both. The only way we can be certain that we are like other people is to engage in a kind of "show-and-tell," where each tells what he happens to know, then the other person does, until they are both bored. But somehow it becomes reassuring.

People often talk—explaining away—just to hear themselves talk. It's usually a monologue that they should have kept private, but they seem unembarrassed to take it public.

Meetings are good examples. People tell the rest of the gathering what they happen to know. They tell stories to embellish their opining. Husbands and wives turn out frequently to have nothing to say to one another. They have professed their love, and the other now knows they are making it up just to hear themselves talk. They either go silent. Or they drive one another crazy with their boring explanations of things.

There is the old adage tossed about by people like Ben Jonson, which is known, in effect, as follows:

They talk and talk, those who cannot think.

That may not be the case. But why does the notion persist over time? Is it that thinkers carry on scintillating conversations with themselves, and those who can't think use television heavily, and like to explain things they know little or nothing about except what they heard or read.

Small children actually want to be astonished. To a child, a world beyond commonplace comprehension is fantastic. And their imaginations run rampant in such incomprehensible worlds.

A few years of schooling will drive that out of them. Adults do not like to be astonished. They offer explanations to guard them from astonishment. Becoming an adult means leaving childish things behind. It is a dire loss to see the world only through rational explanations of things.

The kind of socialization we provide extinguishes the youngster's capacity for wonder and astonishment and replaces it with a capacity to believe in explanation.

We prefer to imbibe fantastic things in our movies and books. We don't want to live there. We just want to experience that vicariously.

If we do not understand something, we just make up a plausible (to others) explanation. Small children learn how to do this quickly, simply by observing adults.

We have a surfeit of explanations about everything under the sun. We add to the stock everyday. We have subcultures that are comprised of people who share the same category of explanations.

The answer to life becomes a statement (an explanation). We've forgotten how to question because we are submerged in a sea of statements (explanations). There is nothing left to be astonished *by*. The experts in various fields will make certain of that. When in doubt, adults do not ask questions. They make a statement intended to explain things.

Explain love or sex to a young child. The legendary Red Grange was once asked how he did what he did—how he was able to slip through so many tacklers on the football field. His reply:

> *"No one ever taught me and I can't teach anyone. If you can't explain it, how can you take credit for it?"*

A provocative perspective. So your explanations give you social credits. His reluctance to make up a proprietary explanation is a breath of fresh air. We are bombarded by made-up explanations 24/7. To explain sex or love to a young child means offering up your received wisdom on those subjects—your own experiences, or what you have heard or read.

Some people just ought not to be explaining things. This is the number two problem after over-population. Explaining things is a form of procreation. It creates every-more explanations of things, exponentially.

Most people over-explain things, and are over-explained to. Over-explaining is just a bad habit developed over years of practice.

> *"Talk,"* as the Chinese proverb has it, *"does not cook rice."*

This may suggest that talk doesn't in itself accomplish anything of value utility—except of course more talk. We are drowning in our talk, talk, talk, as Lewis Carroll's Walrus said.

The playwright Euripides wrote in the Bacchae (c. 407 B.C.):

> *"Talk sense to a fool and he calls you foolish."*

Thinking about this might well remind us—whoever hears us always has the absolute prerogative of making sense of what we say out of his own interpretations, a function of his own mind. It often happens in our world that a foolish person is taken to be a genius of some sort.

We are not constrained by what people say—except by social politics. We do not necessarily follow wise men and women. We follow celebrity and fashion. *Their* explanations count.

Finally, we may take note of Thoreau's observation, in *Walden* (1854):

> *"I should not talk so much about myself if there were anybody else whom I knew as well."*

We explain what is familiar to us. What could be more familiar than one's own explanations of things?

The Interlocutors of Our Lives

This is an old vaudeville term. It referred to the person who explained to the audience what was going on, and to the players on stage what the next transition was to be. Vaudeville acts were largely unrelated to each other. The course of our lives would be also if we did not have those who make a coherent (or comprehensible) story out of what is really fortuitous—our own lives.

So I'm using this term to identify the people or the stories that make our own lives seem coherent. Things are explained in a way that can make our lives seem coherent. These explanations translate the world for us. And they translate us for the rest of the world.

An interlocutor is a *connector*. He can be a story teller, who connects us to the virtual world of the teller, and connects the virtual world of others with us. The process connects us with ourselves.

We become conscious of who we are. We always have the feeling—as a result of how we got it—that the world *we* see is the one that other people see.

Parents first and then teachers are interlocutors. Friends are interlocutors. The authors of the books we read and the radio and television programs we consume are interlocutors. The newspapers that feed our daily habits are interlocutors. Reporters and journalists are interlocutors. Sports announcers and commentators are interlocutors.

An aspect of our celebrity- and expert-worship is that they connect us with worlds we have no access to. Fairy tales and science fiction tales are interlocutors. The adventures of the folk on *Star Trek* are interlocutors.

Interlocutors take us to places we haven't been, or could not go. They take us into space and into ourselves. Love stories, crime stories, hospital stories, and "current events" ("the news") are the leading genres.

Designers and architects are interlocutors, as are forensic experts, archaeologists, historians, preachers, defense lawyers, medical specialists, weather prognosticators, and computer "geeks."

Artists are interlocutors. They enable us to see the world the ways they see the world.

When people tell us stories about themselves, they are functioning as interlocutors. We can have no other access to their thoughts or feelings, unless we ask other people to explain them to us. When people tell us how they see the world, they are creating glimpses of a virtual world that is not our own.

The most prevalent interlocutor is none other than oneself. When we begin talking to ourselves, the interlocutor is that other voice we engage. Let us refer to that other voice as the voice of our consciences, powered by our imaginations.

That other voice is a pure mental fiction, of course. But it is powerful. It can lead us. But it can *mislead* us. When the world is too much with us, or when it is perplexing, we go inside to consult with our consciences. If we have trained and disciplined them, they will work for us. If we haven't, they are as likely as not to work against us.

It is that other voice that needs to be developed. It needs to be purposive. It needs to be more intelligent—and more dedicated—than we are ourselves. It is largely not considered in the socialization of children by parents and teachers. It should be the first consideration, as Thomas Jefferson said.

For heads of state or of organizations or institutions, this is the port of last call for advice. The best leaders are always those who can ultimately count on their own counsel, even though they may listen to many others.

Other people are inescapably a part of our thinking. They will always be there to explain things to us, or even to explain us. Carefully chosen, they can make a contribution to our lives and our aims in life. Carelessly chosen, they can ruin our lives.

Others can ruin our lives. But it takes our imprimatur to make it happen. And we can do it better than they can, as Freud suggested.

The media can help to ruin the lives of people who are diligent consumers.

We can see and hear the talking heads. But the persons who wrote the script or held the camera are invisible. They have their own agendas. Because they are unknown to us, we can only guess what those agendas may be.

All reporting and all journalism function as broad-gauge interlocutors. Commentators inform us 24/7 about what is going on in the world (according to them). Professors profess. Pundits pave the way for our mental pathways.

We like to believe that we more or less run our own lives. We don't. Our lives are run by how we think about things. And how we think about things depends upon who over time has most colonized our minds. The inside and outside worlds are mediated by people we don't—can't—know. So-called *human nature* is a product of how things get explained to us, and what we make of it when we talk to ourselves.

Commercial advertising, for example, explains what we need, what's wrong with us, or what we ought to want. Then (the classic form) it tells us what we ought to do to alleviate our shortcomings, usually what we ought to buy to fix our vain longings.

Those in the media either assume or try to find out what our virtual worlds are like. They prey upon us through the channels we open to them.

The individual remains the key. But there are always others who influence us one way or another. It used to be that people mediated their own worlds because they were in direct contact with them. Now they are mediated by anonymous forces imperceptible to us.

In a way, over time they tell us who we are, what we should do, and even more subtly, how we should think and feel.

They explain things to us. We cannot reciprocate as we can try to with other people. That's the nature of the beast.

Queen Victoria, in an 1859 letter about newspapers, wrote:

> *"None of the worst French novels from which careful parents try to protect their children can be as bad as what is daily brought and laid upon the breakfast-table of every educated family in England, and its effect must be most pernicious to the public morals of the country."*

Rudyard Kipling made this observation on the media around 1831:

> *"Power without responsibility: the prerogative of the harlot throughout the ages."*

Gore Vidal in *Nova* (1968):

> *"The aim of so much journalism is to exploit the moral prejudices of the reader. To say nothing of those of the proprietor."*

Frank Zappa's comment (c. 1980):

> *"Rock journalism is people who can't write interviewing people who can't talk for people who can't read."*

Paddy Chayefsky, the famous script-writer, had a character in the film *Network* (1976) put it this way about television:

> *"Television is an amusement park . . . We're in the boredom-killing business."*

And it was Sam Goldwyn who once quipped,

> *"Why should people go out to see bad movies when they can stay home and see bad television for nothing."*

The *New York Times* writer explained how politicians do it:

> *"The conversation of politics is now carried on in the vernacular of advertising. The big sell, the television sell, appears to be the only way to sell. Increasingly, and especially in Washington, how well one does on television has come to determine how well one does in life."*

With its tentacles architecting most people's minds—as the media go, so goes the civilization. That may seem inevitable, but only to the victims.

The serious and informed critiques never make it on the news. One does not gossip about what will save us. We share our problems, not our dreams. And no dream can come true without the competence to make it happen.

We may be explaining the wrong things to the wrong people.

4

Fault Lines

"Beware of the man who works hard to learn something, learns it and finds himself no wiser than before. He is full of murderous resentment of people who are ignorant without having come to their ignorance the hard way."

—Kurt Vonnegut

The astute observer and writer Kurt Vonnegut is alerting us to the proposition that people who are industrious but manage only to get by are resentful of people who are not industrious but still manage to get by. They may even be "happier," whatever that may mean.

Those who are intellectually ambitious are trying to get ahead but become no wiser for all their effort. Those who are indifferent to their ignorance may in the end be the wiser.

Vonnegut's explanation of this perverse paradox is playful, which is his forte. It is humorous, which is not intended to mean that it is not the way things actually *are*.

One thing that correlates nicely with extended education is mental illness. We like to think such frailties are reserved for the poor and the marginal people of our society. Just the opposite.

Vonnegut is complaining (with tongue in cheek) that such industrious people are keenly resentful of those ignorant folk who did not "come to their ignorance the hard way." Both ended up ignorant, but about different matters.

Ignorant people are not writers. They are not scientists. They may be politicians, but ostensibly not for that reason. They are not the ones who pass judgment on others—unless those others happen to be *intellectuals*.

Prejudice and envy and status-jostling make the world go 'round. Society is structured around such comparative superiority-inferiority, whether based upon money or intellectual capability or position.

Depending on which camp they're in at the moment, people explain things differently. They even concern themselves with explaining different things, on the belief that certain things are inherently more important than other things.

Sailors may know how to tie knots that others can't. But they are unlikely to be granted tenure in any university for that. Professors prattle on and (some) students take notes industriously. Neither the prattle nor the industriousness of capturing it guarantees wisdom or a superior future.

What we want to get into in this chapter are matters like who succeeds and who fails—and why? Every person who experiences the one or the other has an explanation. A few people may intend to outpace, but the mass of people who never make the effort to succeed have a different explanation of such things.

At the heart of conflicting explanations are certain hard-core beliefs about what accounts for what—what *causes* what? And whose fault *is* what happens? In a later chapter, we will bring in the matter of chance in all human and social life. But here we want to tease out why different mental models of explaining why the world works as it does sometimes lead to radically different perspectives on that "same" world.

Who's at Fault?

The simplest cases first.

Human civilization probably began when the first human asked, "WHY?" Why did that happen? And who or what shall we blame?

Blaming and fault-finding are typically the ultimate end of explaining things. If you misbehave in others' eyes, you may try to explain yourself. If others misbehave in your eyes, you may assume they owe you an explanation. They may try a plausible explanation that deflects the blame from them, just as you might.

People use the algorithms that are implicit in their virtual realities to justify themselves and challenge others. People are supposed to think and feel and behave in a certain manner—given the circumstances. If they don't, and if they don't blow the whistle on themselves, someone else is likely to do so.

We always begin with an explanation of what causes what. And then we assess the people and the happenings of the world in terms of the explanations that we apply.

Somewhere, Thoreau wrote:

> "If he is weak in the knees, let him not call the hill steep."

For our purposes, it is an apt metaphor. It suggests immediately that all explanations are subjectively colored. A person can say, "The hill is too steep." But whether it is or not may depend upon how well conditioned that person is to climb it.

A student may say, "This assignment is too difficult." But whether it is or not depends upon how qualified the student is to undertake the assignment.

A lover may say, "I have a headache." But whether that is the case may depend upon many factors other than the reported one.

A subordinate may say, "I didn't complete the project, but there wasn't enough time." That's possible. But the time required to carry out the project also depends upon how competent the person is to carry it out.

An explanation may in fact be an excuse. It may be an opportunity to try to place the blame elsewhere. An explanation may reveal many things. But it does not reveal the *truth* about whatever is being referred to.

People can assert, and usually do. But that does not guarantee the validity of what they say.

That's the simple version. A mid-range version has to do with the erosion of truth between or among people. If people are permitted to escape accountability by explaining away their complicity in an event, they may come to rely more on their ability to explain their way out of problems than on developing the competencies required to dispatch their responsibilities. Those who can rely on their explanations may come to prefer them to the hard work that precludes the need for explanations.

The most complex version of Thoreau's comment is that a society may have favored explanations that are detrimental to it in one way or another. A religious sect that forbids procreation might eventually cease to exist, for example.

Perhaps only by hindsight, but explanations can lead or mislead a person or a whole civilization. Explanations have no taste or smell. They rely completely on belief. If you believe in how you explain things, you will reap the consequences, good or bad. If you are closed to contradictory ways of explaining things, you may miss the opportunity to see the world in a more beneficial way.

Nature in no way is aware of what *causes* what. That is a purely human invention. In the natural world, there is no fault, no laying of blame. Those, too, are purely human inventions.

Every society believes that its way of explaining things is the right or the true way. Present conflicts and wars are struggles to determine whose ways of explaining things are to take precedence. Terrorists have different ways of explaining things than do their victims.

So it is far from being a trivial matter—this business of explaining things. Spouses fight about whose way of explaining things is to prevail. So do nations.

What "Causes" What?

Human societies are built out of explanations about what was, is, or would be the cause of what. "Causation" is at the heart of how we explain our past, our present, and our future.

what caused what? In the present: what is the cause of these
es? In the future: if we do this it will cause this result in the
future.

We are ourselves, we believe, caused by this or that. The world is as it
is because it was caused to be that way. We could be the cause of tomorrow,
but it is far more likely that tomorrow will be the *cause* of us.

And yet we also believe that we could be the cause of who we are in the
future. Science has its cause-and-effect dominance in our culture. We like
it. It simplifies things. The explanations are all rational. They are also put
forward as being more or less *inevitable*.

We believe and explain things one way in public. But we secretly want to
believe the opposite. Children were told at one time not so long ago that
they could be anything they wanted to be. Why this was patently not true
for the parents and teachers but was preached as if true for the children
remains to be explained.

> *Almost all explanations seem to exempt the explainer.*

This causes *that* is an algorithm. You can work it both ways. You can try
to sleuth out the this that caused that. Or you can start with the that (the
effect) and conjure up the this (the cause). Life is lived both ways. You can
explain how you got to be the way you are. Or, you can imagine the person
you want to be and invent some causes.

In that perverse way, the imagined effect can become the *cause* of what is
said or done.

> If you can imagine a plausible and satisfactory explanation
> (in the eyes of others) *for doing or not doing something,* then
> *the explanation becomes the* motive *for your talk or your*
> *behavior.*

You can put any kind of spin you want on your talk or behavior as long as you
can explain it in a way others will accept. Love is like that. So is advertising.
So is politics. In short, so is everyday life in any society.

In the *Purgatorio* section of *The Divine Comedy* (c.1310-1321), Dante Alighieri wrote this fecund line:

". . . if the present world go astray, the cause is in you, in you it is to be sought."

Again, it is but a metaphor. But a potent one. What he is saying (and how would we ever know for sure, since we cannot ask him to explain?) is that "as you explain things, so shall you *be*." The cause is not you, but in you. It is in the way you explain things. It is in how your culture explains things—which is still you, since you are ultimately free to create your own explanations.

Your culture's explanations of things can take you right to hell. But so can your own explanations. It is the crucible of human life that we get to choose. We might even invent explanations of things that take us to paradise rather than to hell.

A provocative parallel exists in the playwright Sophocles' *Oedipus Rex* (c. 430 B.C.):

"The greatest griefs are those we cause ourselves."

The "we" here can refer to us as individuals or to the virtual reality we inhabit in the cultures we live in. Either way, he says, those griefs are those we cause ourselves—directly or indirectly, as by complicity for example. Those who do not choose for themselves have the same destiny as the culture they inhabit. The Roman Empire might be an object lesson for the latter, as would our own civilization.

The lesson is this, again: *As we explain ourselves and the world we inhabit, so shall we BE.*

Explaining things always has the inevitable consequence of being a self-fulfilling prophecy. We become what is implicit in our explanations of things. So beware how you—we—explain things, for those explanations will have real consequences for you and for us.

Here is yet another angle to consider. The clever commentator on modern life, Alexander Woolcott, wrote in 1943 (the year of his death):

> "*Germany was the cause of Hitler just as much as Chicago is responsible for the* Chicago Tribune."

Hitler has been much maligned for the unconscionable deeds that occurred during his time in office. But we have to remember—or do we?—that he was elected to his office by the German people. And he may have considered that for everything he did (as a result of his fawning popularity as a politician) he had a mandate from his people to do what was done.

History is not made up of isolated events. All events have a history as well. Abraham Lincoln could not have done what he did if the "South" had not done what it did.

Whatever is done is always done in a context that reaches back to conflicting explanations, and forward toward conflicting expectations. The person in charge might be a hero. But he or she is more likely to be a victim—of the times, of the circumstances, or of what else was going on.

Jack Welch, for example, may have looked good. But could he have done what he did in bad economic times? Barack Obama may not look so good as a leader in the current circumstances. But if times were good, would we explain him differently?

Everyone who has ever been the one in charge—from parents to presidents to emperors—has had to face this dilemma. Their critics have the advantage of hindsight, which they did not have. It's likely most could be successful as the one in charge if they had the advantage of hindsight as foresight.

But choices and decisions are always made out of uncertain foresight. And things happen along the way that change the context—slightly or critically.

What causes what? may work in a laboratory where the context is controlled. But life is not lived in a laboratory. It is lived in an ongoing cauldron of happenings and counter-happenings and collateral happenings. The context is ever-changing.

Cause-and-effect may simplify things. But that may just be its shortcoming.

"Theories" and Things

In his recent book, *Wrong*, science and business journalist David H. Freeman provides us with the facts about why experts like scientists, finance wizards, doctors, relationship gurus, and even journalists keep failing us. And, one might assume, parents and teachers and friends, who can do more damage in one day than the experts can do in a month. The crux of the matter: the experts don't agree.

Things here refers to research and authoritative pronouncements of all sorts. And "theories" refers mainly to the anecdotal machinations of people's minds that lead them to explain things the way they see it, or to readily accept others' theories as they might be offered in media advertising or in casual gossip. We see what we see through our own comprehensions. And we believe what we believe because our ways of explaining things (our "theories") justify our beliefs.

Authoritative pronouncements may be well-intentioned. But researchers choose their facts and their procedures, just like politicians do. No one is innocent, and no one is particularly guilty of any wrong-doing. It has come to be just the way we do things in our culture.

It has long been known that a philosopher will lie to you for his own advantage. So will a lover. And so will your friends and your favorite celebrities.

Science builds grand theories out of facts. It is their theories that select for them the facts they will pay attention to, as Einstein said. But in a world which is forever reaching out for a better "truth," there will always arise a *better* truth.

The new truth falsifies the old truth. That's why we and our experts eventually turn out to be wrong. Lovers vow to love one another *forever* and that may hold until they start explaining things differently to themselves—for whatever reason.

It is a theory that converts a person into a lover. That theory is subject to revision when different explanations come along to displace the old ones.

The young Winston Churchill wrote (in 1898):

> *"I pass with relief from the tossing sea of Cause and*
> *Theory to the firm ground of Result and Fact."*

Explanations of cause are always changing. Theories are ultimately in place only to be refuted. But results are not so fickle. They are not talk. They are tangible fact. The facts we merely talk about are not real. But the results are.

The firm ground Churchill alludes to lies in making oneself subordinate to the results. Science—and people in general these days, co-opted as they are by science—try to make the results subordinate to them. It's the wrong way around. It comes from the wrong way of explaining things.

We moderns have a lust for technology—the newer the better. We got there by how things were explained in the near past.

But now, increasingly, technology explains the world to us. It even explains us to ourselves. We have to subordinate ourselves as humans to our technological devices in order for them to work. But technologies are not a result of anything but the ingenuity and effort to make them. They are not themselves *human* results. They were not invented to humanize us. They may not have been invented to *de-humanize* us, but they do.

We have gone from worshipping the gods to worshipping our technologies. We have allowed our futures not to lie with us, but with our technologies. They now explain things to us.

Whose fault is that—if fault it be? Whose? It is everyone's and no one's. It is a fault line in humanity. We explained things in ways that now take away our prerogative to explain things.

Maybe that's the way it should be.

If so, what was *Humanism* all about?

Destiny or Destination?

Destiny is fate. We end up in the direction we are going—à la evolution, for example. Destiny is inevitable, whether controlled by the gods or by our tools and technologies—something outside ourselves.

Destination implies *choice*. Our destiny is created for us by other forces. Don Quixote *chose* his values, his beliefs. They were not chosen for him. That he appears ludicrous to many moderns only bespeaks our willingness to let things be in charge, to barter our choices for our toys. We're just along for the ride.

It would probably be fair to say we are no longer much concerned about either our destiny or our destination. We're *modern*. We want ours here and NOW.

Native Americans thought it was imperative to make judgments that would be good for five generations to come. It would be unusual for the typical American today to think ahead even one year. Young people seem to prefer to think ahead only about a day or two—or to the next big event. We punctuate our lives with happenings, not with choice.

We simply explain our lives differently. Whether that is better for us or for our progeny is a non-issue—to most people. We indulge ourselves at the moment because, as the ad saying goes, "We deserve it."

So we focus on what we deserve, with little concern for the future of our civilization, or ourselves. We justify our own needs, not those of our own future or of future generations. Politicians have to play that game even to get elected. We spend more time on our faces than we do on our future.

We don't want to *become* anything in particular. We just want to be "happy." And, as we explain it, that is due us NOW.

Living Faultlessly

The observer and writer ("explainer") Stanislaw Lec offered this prescient metaphor in his *More Unkempt Thoughts* (1968):

> *"No snowflake in an avalanche ever feels responsible."*

The more people there are, the more we rush together headlong into whatever the future holds for us. If we're moving solidly with the masses, we have no sense of responsibility for what happens.

The forces that seem to be controlling us are anonymous. We become anonymous. So how can "anonymous" be responsible?

We hide in the crowd, while asserting our unique individuality. We do what we want. The results are someone else's responsibility.

We didn't know what we were making when we made ourselves "modern."

The famous existentialist ("explainer") Jean Paul Sartre wrote in 1939:

> *". . . yet we are responsible for what we are—that is the fact."*

That may be. But what is one snowflake in an avalanche going to do about *that*?

We have a sense of helplessness. Is that because we have explained ourselves into a state of helplessness? Where the majority rules, the naysayers have little more than irritating voices.

Our way of explaining things has brought us to a world in which being fashionable is far more important than being right. It is a world in which we want the right to explain ourselves however we wish, and in whatever ways are currently fashionable.

But we abstain from responsibility for the consequences—whatever they may be.

Some people think that explaining things is a mere parlor game. They abjure the potency of every utterance, every understanding. How did we come to explain things that way?

It may be the way we have come to explain it in our culture. But there is no such thing as explanation without far-reaching and even unpredictable consequences.

5

Comprehending

> *"Physics tries to discover the pattern of events which controls the phenomena we observe. But we can never know what this pattern means or how it originates; and even if some superior intelligence were to tell us, we should find the explanation unintelligible."*
>
> —Sir James Hopwood Jeans
> (in *Physics and Philosophy*, 1942)

Every infant recapitulates humanity. At first, everything is incomprehensible. Each has to learn what and how to comprehend whatever its immediate culture considers to be comprehensible.

Comprehending is a more proactive word than understanding, although they could be taken to mean roughly the same thing. To understand something is a passive term. Comprehending implies a complex dynamic, an ongoing active involvement.

The process is one of transforming the incomprehensible (via explanation) into the comprehensible. None of this is random or arbitrary. There is first the matter of *what* is to be made comprehensible. Then it is a matter of how to explain it so that it is comprehensible.

Jeans uses the word unintelligible instead of incomprehensible. That may have been purely stylistic. But it could be taken to mean "not intelligible to the limited intelligence we put up against it." That is, there is nothing that is universally intelligible. It depends. It depends upon what manner of intellect is used to transform what *isn't* into what *is* intelligible.

No cultural group comprehends everything. Certain things are deemed important, certain other things are deemed unimportant, and there are still other things that people in general will be blind to all of their lives.

Comprehending is like staking a claim on the world. The things we explain become our territory, so to speak. The things we cannot—or do not—explain remain the unknown to us.

Our particular brand of science would like to explain everything, and attempts to do so. But ignorance increases at the same rate that knowledge increases. There will always be more that we do *not* understand than we do understand. Human knowledge is like an island surrounded by the unknown. As the island grows, the shoreline grows.

Knowledge is a group thing. What one group believes is worth knowing, another group may be oblivious to.

As far as humanity is concerned, our reach will always exceed our grasp. We invent as many stories to explain ourselves to ourselves as any ancient peoples did. Or, even more.

We may reach and reach. But that does not enlarge our grasp. That will always be limited. The intelligence we bring to bear is merely the intelligence that *we* bring to bear.

We only explain the things we explain. That's all we can really claim. What is comprehensible to us is not the world. It is merely the virtual world we create in our ambitious but simplistic explanations of it.

We know who we are because our explanations tell us so. We know what is what and supposedly what causes what because our explanations tell us so. But, as Jeans suggested, we cannot know what all of that is supposed to *mean* to us. And, if we were told by someone of superior intelligence to us, that explanation would be unintelligible—to us.

Minding "a World"

It may seem an awkward term, *minding*. And it may not be in your dictionary. I know it is not in mine. But I hear words every day that are not in my dictionary.

Still, we need this word. It speaks to what we pay attention to—to what we are capable of paying attention to, to what is readily comprehensible to us, and what is beyond the reach of our understanding. It speaks to the process of admitting into our minds what is intelligible to us, and being oblivious to all the rest. It speaks to the fact that our minds are not really so much a "thing" as a set of processes.

Minding is something that is going on every minute of every day. It is the source of our consciousness, and our self-consciousness. It is backed up by what we know and have known, what we feel and have felt, what we believe and what we don't.

Minding is a very individual and impenetrable sequence of acts (to others, or even to ourselves). We can tune in, but our minding goes about its business quite independently of any volition on our part. It is quite personal and private. But minds collude with each other. And our own private minds end up functioning quite like those around us.

We can think. We can think we think. But it is our minding that does this for us. Without minds, we would have no concept of thinking. And yet we don't actually micro-manage our thinking. Our minding goes on and on autonomously, doing its own thing.

It is the source of conscious awareness, of what we are capable of hearing or reading, and of what we are capable of expressing to ourselves and to others.

This minding business is a fierce slave that becomes the master, like the genie. We live by it. It takes us where *it* goes. Once set in motion—the minding part of it—it does not do what we want it to do. We do what it permits and facilitates, what it makes possible and what it makes impossible.

That's part of it. The other part of it is even more important.

It is that we do not mind THE world. We mind *A* world—the virtual world that we carry with us wherever we go, whatever is going on. We do not—cannot—mind THE world. We can only mind the virtual world that our *minding* makes possible and necessary. *Mind* is a verb.

So when people are talking about "the" world, they are not talking about "it," they are talking about their particular version of it, given in how they have come to mind it. We do not mind any actual world. We mind our interpretations of it. It is those myriad interpretations that are the warp and weft of our minding of the *virtual world* we inhabit mentally and emotionally.

From the *Dhammapada* section of The Pali Canon (the sacred scriptures of Theravada Buddhists, c.500—c.250 B.C.) we have this cryptic lesson:

> *"All that **is** comes from the mind; it is based on the mind,*
> *it is fashioned by the mind."*

The infrastructure of all conscious life is our minding of the world. All we see, all we feel, all we know comes from the mind. It is the core of human *being*. It is minds in action that composes not just all intellectual activity, but all social activity.

What we comprehend is given by our minding of it—not by *it*. Our minding of the world is not regulated or constrained by the world. We are free to explain things as might be possible and necessary in the culture we belong to. There is no sense in which it is mandated that we will comprehend the world as it is. Nor is the world obligated to be the way we explain things.

Comprehending anything at all is a function of however we have come to mind it. The boundaries of our comprehending are the boundaries of our world. We live in and through our minding. That to which we pay no heed may destroy us. But it is our explanations of things by which we navigate.

The Incomprehensible

What is incomprehensible to us is like an itch. We have to scratch it. We might say that humans exist (or that human minds exist) to transform the incomprehensible into the comprehensible. We do this by whatever means may be available. We create myths. We make up stories. We invent theories. We invent gods to explain things we can't understand to us. We paint. We dance. We play music. We explain things to one another—no matter how wayward our explanations may be.

If we want to grasp the incomprehensible, we have to make it comprehensible. One way or another, we will create a way of explaining it—if we believe it to be important to our ways in the world.

The universal human motive has always been that of making comprehensible to ourselves whatever is incomprehensible. Our dreams are often incomprehensible. But we even make up *some* way to "explain" *them*.

In an 1810 letter to Bettina von Arnim, Beethoven wrote,

> "Art! Who comprehends her? With whom can one
> consult concerning this great goddess?"

With whom, indeed? The only people who really comprehend art (in their own ways) are those who create art. The part of great art that we don't understand, as the artist Braque said, is the part we can't explain. All the rest of us make up some explanation or another, and we nod approvingly when others accept or confirm our explanations.

We invent a way of comprehending. What we comprehend is the way in which we have explained art—not the art itself or the artist himself.

Beethoven was right. Yet what he said about art would be true of love or of freedom or of how to live. We consult with one another and come up with an explanation that makes comprehensible whatever it is we want to talk about.

That rascally fellow Machiavelli had this to say about comprehension (in *The Prince*, c. 1532):

> "There are three classes of intellects: one which comprehends
> by itself; another which appreciates what others comprehend;
> and a third which neither comprehends by itself or by the
> showing of others; the first is the most excellent, the second
> is good, the third is useless."

That leaves open how much uselessness there is in our present culture.

Nonetheless, it is worth noting carefully that people vary greatly in their capacity for comprehension. We sometimes take the faulty position that people are more or less equal—at least interchangeable—in their capacity for comprehension, and that the world is there for everyone to observe . . . equally and identically.

That is not possible—never has been, and probably never will be. Machiavelli's is an observation that has been made over all of human history. If some people are smart, then some people are stupid. If some people grasp the world in broader and deeper ways, then some people can grasp the world only in myopic and thinner ways.

No one is born with the capacity for comprehending the virtual world that people have made and continue to make in their talk about it. You have to be able to talk and to understand other people's talk. You have to *participate* in that human-made virtual world of the mind in order to comprehend any world at all.

Comprehending Oneself

It is impossible to comprehend oneself without comprehending others, or without being comprehended by others. Even so, how we comprehend ourselves is central to the lives we have.

Initially, we have no choice but to see ourselves as those around us see us. They call us by the names they gave us. We had no say in that. They explain to us all the things they want us to comprehend, including ourselves. We had little say in that.

The question, "Who *am* I?" (or even "*What* am I?") occurs with the dawning of self-consciousness, and hangs around as a lifelong work in progress for many people all their lives.

We are constructed first of all out of how others express their comprehension of us. With self-consciousness comes the opportunity to fiddle around with that—to be one of the co-authors of who we are.

Who we *are* is some amalgam of how others explain to us in one way or another who we are, and of our own fictions about who we imagine we are. Those who struggle to achieve in any field of endeavor or in life must necessarily take over the explaining business and become the primary if not the dominant author of who they intend to be.

The risk for achievers is that they may become less and less cognizant of how others explain or define them. In taking over the reins of their lives, they may lose sight of how others see them. This can often be to their detriment. The amalgam of one's own and others' comprehensions is a necessary ingredient of life. If you want to change others comprehensions, you must figure out how to change their minds via your communication with them, and your behavior in their perceptions of you.

Only fragments of the Greek philosopher Heraclitus' writings survived. (He's the "You can't step in the same river twice" guy—c. 540-480 B.C.) One fragment that might provide some insight here is:

"Much learning does not teach understanding."

We assume that it does. But we also assume that learning and education are the same thing. They are not.

Ideally, perhaps, education provides us with the answers and a handful of lawful algorithms. Learning, by contrast, enables more learning. Learning begins with questions—questions about things that baffle us, about things we know little or nothing, questions about what is more or less incomprehensible to us at the moment.

Most learning is incidental. It occurs adventitiously. Something inside or outside of us happens. We wonder about it. That leads to learning. We *grow* our active minds by our learning. We learn only some uncertain facts by education.

So my guess is that Heraclitus is here referring to what we now call education. And indeed it seems that the more education modern people are subjected to, the *less* they understand of what they are most in need of understanding. Extended education also correlates nicely with mental dysfunctions of various kinds.

It is wonder and puzzlement that lead to understanding—to richer comprehension.

That venerable philosopher, statesman, and scientific thinker Sir Francis Bacon wrote in his *Aphorisms*:

> *"The human understanding is like a false mirror, which . . .*
> *distorts and discolors the nature of things by mingling*
> *its own nature with it."*

By its own nature, Bacon was referring to the virtual worlds that people have constructed for themselves by explaining everything.

He wrote that in 1620. Since then, the virtual world has virtually eclipsed the nature of things as the world we inhabit. So the false mirror works both ways. Today, we are more likely to take the position that the way we have come to see the world is the given, and the nature of things distorts and discolors our understanding. So we intend to fix the world (the nature of things) until *it* is as we humans have come to comprehend it.

So the way the human understanding "distorts and discolors the nature of things" is not merely a quaint idea. It is our prerogative and our mandate to do so. We are to take dominion over the nature of things by explaining them for our purposes.

How we comprehend ourselves is always a function of how we comprehend everything else we want to talk about—or to explain. The mirror is now the way we have explained and continue to explain things. We see ourselves and invent ourselves in *that* mirror.

"The nature of things" is always a player. But it is something we would like to eliminate. If the planet is warming or cooling, our illusion is that we are responsible for that and need to fix it.

There are very few people who concern themselves with the nature of things. That's simply how they comprehend themselves. But the rest of us have our lives in how we explain ourselves to others, and how they explain themselves to us. Our problems come from the trust required by those relationships.

And from the fact that the only people who can betray us are those we trust. We have built a whole world independent of the actual nature of things.

Even when we try to explain *that*, we reveal more about ourselves than we do about that. To comprehend ourselves, we have to stand on what is tacit in our explanations of ourselves. It was a trap. Physicists some time ago realized that what they observed was modified by the very act of their observing.

It is the same for attempting to comprehend ourselves. We necessarily modify ourselves in trying to do so.

Comprehending and Believing

It is easy for people to comprehend what they already believe. It is not so easy to comprehend those people who believe differently.

If you don't believe that, try talking someone who deeply dislikes you into being your lover. Or someone whose identity hinges upon your not being who you are.

People are *relevant* to other people (the fundamental social motive)because their comprehensions of one another are mutually suitable (or advantageous). If I need you and you need me, we have a working relationship. If I love you and you hate me, we don't. If our beliefs are compatible, then our comprehensions of each other will be compatible.

If I believe you are deceitful, then that is how I will comprehend you. If I trust you, then that is how I will see you. If you comprehend me as trusting you, this opens up for you two options: either to reciprocate the trust, or to take advantage of it.

If you believe in your god, fine. But if you try to convince me that I should have the same belief, we may have a problem. If you believe that you are "right" and therefore that I am "wrong," we have a problem. If you believe that your cereal is superior and mine is inferior, we might have a problem. If the celebrity in whom you believe says "X," and mine says "Y," we could have a problem.

If you base your beliefs on what you have read, as Machiavelli suggested, and another doesn't read because his mind is already made up, you could have a problem. If your beliefs are non-negotiable, but you assume my beliefs should be negotiable, we could have a problem.

And so on. Beliefs precede perception, for most people most of the time. Thus such conflicts in understanding fill the small stage of everyday life and the larger stages of international and intercultural life perpetually.

We believe there should be rational means for resolving them. But we would be wrong. Beliefs are not acquired by rational means. And they are not likely to be dislodged by rational arguments.

We got them because we bought into some explanation of things—whether about us or the shifting sands of the world around us. Once "bought," now owned. They become a possession we are loathe to part with.

The Morality of Comprehending

This has been an issue for philosophers and other thinkers from the beginning.

It was explained—even in our own Bible—that knowing things we shouldn't know was sinful. After all, Adam and Eve got expelled from Paradise because they comprehended some things they were not supposed to. Eating of the fruit of the tree of knowledge was what led to their—and presumably—our destiny.

There is something to this. We have this proverb:

"Familiarity breeds contempt."

Before lovers "know" the other person, they are full of wonder and awe. That wears off with the details that come with familiarity.

It is only people who know another person intimately who can really hurt that other person. Strangers might kill you. But intimates can sentence you to a slow death.

Behind it all is this:

There is no observation or understanding that is "innocent." If you speak or if you understand, you become complicit in whatever the consequences turn out to be. To speak or to understand signals the loss of innocence—whether for an infant or for a civilization.

Because we understand what has been passed on to us, and because we can talk about it to others, we are complicit in perpetuating the implicit destiny of our tribe. Words have consequences. Understandings have consequences. These affect us directly. They affect our tribe or our civilization indirectly.

We have been forewarned of this for millennia. But we have never really comprehended it, or its implications. Talk (like explaining things) is easy. Coping with the consequences is exceedingly more difficult.

If we have relationship problems—whether at home or at work—we have "psychological" explanations that today makes it seem as if neither of us is to blame. If we have international problems, we have explanations (e.g., "terrorism") that relieve us of any blame. Or, as ex-President Clinton put it,

"It's the economy, stupid."

Most people would be inclined to believe this, in spite of the fact that it was people who invented the economy in the first place and are now complicit in the economy we have to live with.

It is only vaguely comprehensible to most people that those who lived beyond their means did not have some direct complicity in the deep recession we have all had to live with.

This raises the key question: when there are forces for good or ill at work in a world of many millions of people, is any*one* to blame? If some people are doing things—or failing to do things—that affect us all, are they somehow to be held accountable? If some people are working hard and others are not working at all because they are disinclined, is their negative contribution to be held against *them*?

LEE THAYER

Or do we, in our wayward culture, simply find it easier to explain things we don't directly control by some abstraction—like "the economy"?

Ours is not a moralistic culture. It is a legalistic culture. In the name of another abstraction—"freedom"—we are free to do whatever we might want to do. It is someone else's problem to take care of any consequences we may not like.

The 20th-century Swiss theologian Karl Barth put our human-made human predicament this way:

> *"We have before us the fiendishness of business competition and . . . war, passion and wrong-doing, antagonism between classes and moral depravity within them, economic tyranny above and the slave spirit below."*

He is saying, it seems to me, that unless there is a powerful sense of morality on the part of most people, we bring these bad things down on ourselves. We can explain things otherwise. But there doesn't seem to be much evidence that such abstract explanations have helped much to create a better world.

By the slave spirit, he is referring to the sense of helplessness and hopelessness that most people share when this widespread sense of morality doesn't exist. Like slaves, we are resigned to adapt to things over which have no direct control.

We would like to elect a President, or simply to wish for some hero to come along and save us. It has been explained to us that such a thing isn't going to happen.

Apparently, if history is any guide, we cannot be free *and* irresponsible at the same time. We cannot have the kind of world we dream of if we haven't got what it takes to *make* such a world.

The bad news is that it was people explaining things that created the world we live in.

The good news is that *if* we made it wrong, we could—possibly—make it right.

Everyday morality, as George Bernard Shaw put it,

> "... is largely a system of making cheap virtues a cloak
> for expensive vices."

And it is also, of course, a matter of being hypocritical. We (people) talk a good game. But *speaking of bulls is not the same as being in the bullring,* as the Spanish proverb has it. Every politician, like every child, knows that there is no necessary correlation between what is said and what is done. We lie to ourselves and we lie to one another—either in what we say or what we do.

Our epoch has been the grand epoch of discovering our selves, of self-aggrandizement. It isn't an aggrandized self that we need. It's the stuff of which a good and right self is made. If our explanations of things do not ride on the keel of morality, then they will lead us astray.

The last word should probably be given to Evan Esar, the columnist, who subtly gets at the underlying issue of the morality of our comprehending:

> "All of us would gladly accept the advice of our moral
> superiors—the difficulty is to find any."

Without a sense of morality, people take their explanations of things from other people who are as bereft of a sense of morality as they are.

That's a losing game.

6

Justifying

"There are two reasons for doing things—a very good reason and the real reason."

—Anonymous

"Every man is encompassed by a cloud of comforting convictions, which move with him like flies on a summer day."

—Bertrand Russell

What we do will either be pre-justified by cultural custom, or we will assume we are capable of justifying what we do to others' satisfaction.

All behavior (including verbal or nonverbal behavior) has to be justified. It is pre-justified in the eye of the beholder *only* if it is so commonly used that it needs no justification. In that case the person performing has guessed rightly that his or her behavior requires no justification. OR, if it appears to others to be outside the norm, they themselves feel justified in blowing the whistle on the one doing the "misbehaving."

At stake here is the fact that in social life no behavior is home free. What is justified by custom will guide most behavior. What isn't justified by custom will be unlikely to occur. What can't be justified won't occur—or if it does, it will be punished in some way.

The governance mechanism in all societies is that of what behavior is permissible in the circumstances, *or* what can be satisfactorily explained.

There will always be someone who will accept an explanation for unacceptable behavior. That someone might be one's friends or one's mother. But there is a gatekeeper before that. A person may convince herself that she is justified in what she has done or is about to do. The ultimate judgment, however, will always be society's.

People with weak or poorly formed consciences will have a lot of explaining to do. So-called normal people are unlikely to need to explain their behavior. They will almost always behave within the cultural norms, within the parameters of what is comprehensible and acceptable.

Yet it is always people who behave outside the cultural norms who change the culture. They might be artists, or composers, or inventors of some other sort. An invention that catches on will always change things from that point on. People in large numbers may ridicule the inventor before that happens but lionize him or her subsequently.

The Anonymous quote at the top of this chapter is intended to provoke some fruitful thinking. It reads:

> *There* are *two reasons for doing things—a very good reason and the real reason.*

The very good reason is one that the person doing things and those observing will take as fully justifiable. So the person doing things offers that reason.

The real reason is always hidden from others. It is private, inaccessible to others. It is frequently not even that obvious to the person doing things. If you take the position that people (including yourself) do what they do because they did, you will be on the right track.

The rest of it is guessing why. The person who did something is always capable of lying by offering any explanation that others will accept. And the guesses that others (or even those doing those things) make can never be fully proved one way or the other.

It's all mind work. There is never a tangible cause. We have to make that up. We'll make up something that satisfies the people involved, no matter how wrong it might be. That's the way the virtual world works.

We will never know for certain what the "real" reason was. We'll just make something up that works—and move on.

Saying What's on Your Mind

People don't often say what's on their minds for three reasons.

The **first** reason is that most people usually don't have much on their minds. And they're not so interested in telling other people what's on their mind as trying to get something into the minds of those others.

We like it when the other people we most often converse with have the same things on their minds as we do on ours. So if we do put something out there, it will more than likely be in order to get it validated. We like local news and gossip. We even like talking about politics and medical problems. We do so to sort out those who we like from those we don't.

The **second** reason is that we have learned to be cautious about doing so. We would like to know in advance that the other person or persons are going to believe we are *justified* in both content and delivery. The more uncertain we are about our own thoughts, the more cautiously we are about telling others what's on our mind.

The **third** reason is that it is frequently a kind of game. We would prefer that others tell us first what's on their minds so we can judge or critique what they say. We know that's what they would do if we were to go first. We would like to predict that they are going to agree with us before we say *anything*. In that case, we would probably like them. Then we can put a spin on what we want to say when our turn comes, so that what's going on in our minds we might consider to be more important.

The best relationships are the ones that are asymmetrical—where the relationship is hierarchical—even though that may change from moment to moment. It helps if there is a teacher for a student, a parent for a child in need, a boss for organizing things for the rest of us.

Totally equal relationships don't work out very well. We're not very good at thinking equally. We do better when we're thinking up or down.

There will always be a hierarchy or pecking order in every human encounter. Chickens in the pen wouldn't have it any other way. We people seem to prefer the hypocrisy of saying we believe in equality, but in practice we often perform in the opposite way. That's why we game it.

In his 1964 book *Les Mots* [The Words], Sartre wrote:

> *"Culture doesn't save anything or anyone, it doesn't justify. But it's a product of man . . . ."*

But we do draw our basic justifications from it. There are emerging or perplexing matters that face us—individually or collectively. We have to create justifications for how to deal with them. New justifications widely used become a part of the culture. That's what Sartre meant by saying that a culture is a human product.

Justifying, like explaining things, is an exclusive human activity, and the culture is its product. But I think Sartre is wrong. Cultures do justify. The culture one lives in sanctions certain behaviors, while other behaviors are considered taboo.

It will not save us from anything. But neither will our explanations—whether justified or not.

Ends and Means

It was the 17th-18th-century poet and aphorist Matthew Prior who gave us the oft-quoted and now proverbial observation that

> *"The ends must justify the means."*

This has been agued by philosophers pro and con since then. So there are plenty of those who disagree that the ends do justify the means.

Still, it is useful to explore some of the implications of the original. What Prior is saying is that the consequences or results of what people set out to do intentionally *must* justify the means employed to carry out the action.

He's assuming that it is about what people do to and with and for each other. Disciplining children, for example, must have results that *justify* the means used to do so.

Severe means should produce an especially worthy result. Punishments should be more or less equivalent to the crime or misdemeanor, and so on.

There used to be—and still is in some cultures—severe punishments for any misdoing. Stealing a loaf of bread could cost you the slicing off of the miscreant hand. Female adulterers had to wear a bright-colored "**A**" emblazoned on the foreheads. "Witches" were burned. Harlots were stoned. Horse thieves were hung. Murderers were murdered. Mentally-defective people were tortured, as were traitors.

Sea-going mutineers were lashed and sometimes thrown overboard. People who seriously violated social codes of conduct became shunned social outcasts.

People were punished for their misdeeds. Children were punished for failing to pay attention in school.

So the concept applies whether you are trying to develop character for the future, or simply punishing someone for his or her misdeeds—as, of course, determined by the customs of the day.

So what kind of punishment or disciplinary action for future benefit is really *justified* by what is done to the miscreant?

Let us take a different look at the culturally-determined relationship between behavior and its justification. We might ask the question, "What is beauty?" That has been defined in many different ways, and there have always been cultural differences. Women in our culture, particularly, will punish themselves by the clothes or shoes they wear, or what they go through to have fashionable hair or body shape. Do these ends justify the means?

Or, men will subject themselves to a working life almost like indentured slaves in order to support a family. Do those ends justify the means? Fewer, but still many, seem to think so.

Athletes intending to compete at the Olympic level will undergo rigorous exercise and sweat and subject themselves to pain and stress to become contestants. Do those ends justify the means?

Artists subject themselves to ostracism and marginality in order to pursue their ideals. Do those ends—which may not even occur—justify the means?

To be rich you might have to subject yourself to an almost maniacal regimen of work and focused attention. Do the ends justify the means?

If what some people will subject themselves to in order to be admitted to heaven would be for others a form of prior punishment for an uncertain result—do such ephemeral ends justify the means?

There is almost nothing humans engage in that does not raise the question of whether or not the ends justify the means.

We don't have to try to arrive at a definitive answer here. It is sufficient to note that

> *all human thought, feelings, and behavior has to be justified in some way, whether before, during, or after. We are not free to do or say as we choose. We can live comfortably only when fully justified. Any thinking, feeling, or behavior that is not or cannot be justified may carry a hefty price tag.*

How one prepares to go into the public is intended to provide a message of one sort or another. Body ornamentation, like other costumes and accessories, are both fashion and communication. Cosmetics deceive. Do the intended ends justify the means?

You don't *have to* have the approval of those in your social circles. But you won't be able to play the games they play if you don't have it.

Telling and Asking

We have been told far more than we have been asked. Our exemplars are typically "tellers." They are rarely incorrigible question-askers. Education is a matter of learning the answers, not how to ask the questions, and we have been over-exposed to that through most of our formative years. So we arrive at adulthood having the habits of telling others what we happen to know, but not of asking productive questions.

The right question at just the right time asked of the right person is powerful. You grow from the effort required to formulate just the right question. They grow from the effort required to figure out how to make an intelligible answer.

Making statements in most social situations is socially-justified. Asking—maybe yes, maybe no. That's because most people are pontificators, not askers. You can't lie by asking a question. Telling affords a myriad of opportunities for lying. A question does not provide much of a cover for hypocrisy or deceit. Mutual statement-slinging does.

Gossip is a form of status-seeking in the guise of supposedly innocent stories about people known in common. So are academic, scientific, and sometimes political arguments a form of status-seeking.

Self-Justification

People are always involved in justifying their own thoughts, beliefs, actions, and feelings. They draw from many sources—fashion, folklore, friends—and increasingly from the media. Women (and men) to whom are pitched expensive cosmetics are told, "You're worth it," or "You deserve it."

Of all of the advertising ploys, the most compelling seems to be connected with deserving this or that. This suggests that people use that criterion regularly in their own self-justification. As in, "I shouldn't indulge myself, but I *deserve* it." Or, "I shouldn't have said that, but he/she had it coming."

What we deserve is dished up hourly by the media. We are exposed to images of what celebrities, or the rich and famous, are doing and what they look like in public. "We" deserve to look that way, or to be that way.

y the things that might present us in public at a status or two higher than *w* actually are. Most people in America are social-climbers. Or they would be if they could afford to be—on credit. This contributes to their living beyond their means. And that of course was a contributing factor in the bubble burst of '08.

Mathematically, the debt—including credit card debt—in this country cannot possibly be paid off. There simply isn't enough income to cover the astronomical amount of debt.

What does this have to do with self-justification? It seems that a sense of deserving more, along with encouragement from the media and the creditors, has led people to buy what might make them seem to be more affluent and more glamorous than they actually are.

This works both ways. The 16th-17th-century philosopher Francis Bacon wrote:

> *"The happiness of the great consists only in thinking how happy others must think them to be."*

These days, we can justify to ourselves having that outlook if we just buy the right cosmetics, the right diet plan, the right toys, and buy into the right neighborhood. Then we too can be "happy" in this way.

We can't all look like the models or the very wealthy. We don't have their genes. And we don't have the kind of money they have to look the way they casually pretend. They are media-produced.

But we can emulate them. Thorstein Veblen considered our propensity for emulation to be the primary economic motive in our modern world.

We can justify to ourselves the attempt to look better and have more than we do. The culture helps out here, by condoning status-seeking.

Your automobile "tells" who you are. So do your clothes and the coif of your hair. So does where you live and where you go to socialize or where you go on vacation.

Everything about us communicates to the person who is interested and can read the signs and signals. And no one is more interested in that than those who beam their advertising at us. They play to our weaknesses and susceptibilities. We have no susceptibilities more basic than our ability to justify to ourselves what it might cost to appear to others the way we fantasize ourselves socially. "We're worth it!"

Having an active *conscience* means referring our desires and appetites for who we are in public to the larger culture. If inappropriate, we refrain from saying or doing what we might be inclined to say or do. If the larger culture we have internalized gives us the green light, we proceed.

But most people these days don't have a very active conscience. Or, if they do, they have it well-trained. The columnist Evan Esar quipped:

> *"Conscience is a voice from within that lots of people do without."*

It is difficult to have two masters—one's immediate interests and a conscience that protects reputation in the long term. We live in the "ME" generation, only purportedly a moral one. An active conscience would help us distinguish between right and wrong. If indulging one's immediate interests and desires is right, then that small contrary voice from within must be wrong.

We can justify anything to ourselves. If those we most associate with exhibit that kind of individualistic freedom, then we will emulate them. And they, us. Then either way it's a matter of the blind leading the blind.

Being "Cool"

Although the dynamic remains the same, the specific rules change. The "rules" are the norms for comportment, dress, values, beliefs, and expression. Depending on the group or subculture you belong to, it has always been deemed better to be in rather than out.

Fashions in all matters human come and go. They come from nowhere, seemingly, and they seemingly go independently of our own volition. They are not subject to our will. But they have the power to dictate how we think like we do, how we act like we do, how we believe like we do, how we dress like we do—and the rest of all matters human.

We can try being "different." But then others might emulate us. What was different at the moment will either become the standard, or will be forgotten.

It's a game you can't win. No matter how individualistic one attempts to be, the immediate context—the cultural fashions of the day—will always be the power player.

Most people will side with the criteria the culture provides. They want to be identified with the winner.

There is a Chinese proverb that reads:

> *"He who defines the terms wins the argument."*

The larger culture and the subculture(s) to which you belong will define the terms generally. The people who are in your immediate social environment will provide further definition. It makes little difference how you define the terms if others define them differently.

"Cool" is what those in your circle define as cool. If you accept their definitions for what is cool, and if you comport yourself accordingly, you will be . . . "cool."

What justifies your behaving in order to appear cool are the expectations that others impose upon you.

You might try a radical performance of yourself. But if that doesn't fly (it does only in the movies), you are stuck with loss of status. Plus, you may be called upon to explain your weird behavior.

Social behavior is most often a function either of pre-ordained explanations, or your ability to justify (to explain satisfactorily) your behavior to others who are in a position to sanction it.

Freakish people always risk social ostracism. They may have much to offer the world and the culture. But most people assume that normative (to them) behavior is natural. Anything outside their beliefs and expectations has to be justified by the explanation offered.

Comforting Convictions

As Bertrand Russell said at the head of this chapter, everyone is encompassed "in a cloud of comforting convictions, which move with him like flies on a summer day."

It is an apt metaphor. Most people have long since acquired their convictions in their early years. What's comforting is that they can apply them with but minor changes for the rest of their lives. They are no longer learners. They now know whatever needs knowing.

As long as they continue on with the kind of people they started with, they will have little need to change in any fundamental way. The rest of life is just cosmetic.

Those convictions are comforting because they are familiar, they require little in the way of maintenance, and they are permanent. The world or the culture may change. But then it would be wrong.

Their convictions remain justified as long as they have enough friends and associates to sanction them. At a certain age, babies and old people don't have to explain their wayward behavior to others, who are culturally obligated to accept it.

Our oft-quoted humorist Evan Esar offered this quip:

> *"The difference between an opinion and a conviction
> is that you hold one, while the other holds you."*

If it weren't for the stubbornness of large numbers of people who live by their convictions, the world would change far more randomly and far more speedily than it does. It is often the arbitrary fashions and beliefs of younger generations that propel the changes that do occur.

A well-worn and culturally-sanctioned algorithm becomes a conviction. *You don't have to explain a conviction to others who are held by the same conviction.*

If you are held by the same convictions as are your fellow-travelers, you have no need to justify who you are or why you behave the way you do.

The underlying struggle is always between change and resistance to change. There is little reason to believe that that basic struggle will ever change. It is the ultimate dynamic of human and social life.

We need both. But how and when? And in what balance? That's why we will always have to *explain things.*

7

Disambiguating

"Explanation consists merely in analyzing our complicated systems into simpler systems in such a way that we recognize, in the complicated system, the interplay of elements already so familiar to us that we accept them as not needing explanation."

—Percy Bridgman, in *The Nature of Physical Theory*

Being human means we have to make what is incomprehensible to us into what is comprehensible to us.

Being verbal means we always have to translate what others express. Their meaning does not pierce our skulls anywhere. They had something in mind. We have to use our own minds to try to figure out what they might have meant by what they expressed or what they did. This is the continuous task of disambiguating others' utterances, their behavior or any other form of expression, like dress or comportment.

We have to learn how to *read* a work of art, or a blueprint, or a financial statement, or even a bank statement. Everything we encounter in life is ambiguous. We take the ambiguity out of it by imposing a meaning on it.

We take those meanings from the active resources of our own minds. Nothing comes to us with its meaning inscribed on its back (or front or intonation). It is our task to *disambiguate* whatever it is that we're not sure we understand.

This is particularly true of what people say or do. All verbalizations are ambiguous. They could be interpreted in different ways. All behavior is ambiguous. It could be interpreted by different people in different ways.

Everything we attend to has to be interpreted—by us. No matter how articulate someone is in what she says, she can always be interpreted in ways not intended.

The ambiguity comes from the fact that we are imperfect communicators on both sides of the equation. That's because there is no way to say or express or do something that can avoid being interpreted by other people—according not to what was expressed or intended, but according to how others happen to interpret it.

This makes for communication problems of all sorts—at home, at work, at play. You **will** be misinterpreted (but only according to you). Such instances are not really misinterpretations. They are merely the receiver's interpretations, which can easily be different from your own.

Thus all communication—in whatever the form or medium—is ambiguous. The outcome is ambiguous to the artist, the politician, the boss, or the parent because the originator can never know for sure what the listener's or viewer's interpretation will be.

It is ambiguous to the listener, the observer, or the viewer because he cannot always know what was meant by what was said, what was done, or what was expressed.

And therein lies the crux of the matter—what does *anything* mean?

Meaning

People deal in the meaning of things. We have no choice. Every human mind traffics in the *meanings* of things—not in the "booming, buzzing" incomprehensibility of actual happenings.

We have to depend wholly on our *minding* of the world. Things are what they mean to us—individually or collectively. They are not, for us, what they actually may be.

Everything has to be translated, converted into whatever those things or events *mean* to us.

Everything is ambiguous until some human *disambiguates* it. This always occurs in some cultural and relationship context. The culture and the relationship are the heavyweights in the process. No interpretation is purely individual. Humans have to disambiguate everything. But they will usually do so according to the cultural recipes of the day for doing so.

Ambiguity has to do with uncertainty about the *meaning* of things. Disambiguating is the process of arriving at an *acceptable* meaning. It may not be the right one, or a valid one. Any interpretation works so long as it satisfies people's immediate uncertainty.

Words and Meanings

Meaning does not rely on words—or even on images or numbers or scientific formulae. All meanings rely on persons. It is people who impose meanings on things. Those meanings are not a product of the event. They are a product of the person observing.

In his *Four Quartets* (1935), the poet T. S. Eliot referred to the

> "... *intolerable wrestle*
> *With words and meanings.*"

It is not just "words." Anything that requires human interpretation, which is everything—from behavior to paintings, music, movies, dress, and conversations—involves a sort of *code* that has to be decoded. We have to learn how to read a painting. We have to learn how to listen to music and get it. We have to learn how to encode in words, and decode words. We have to learn how to *decode* the world we live in, however and wherever we encounter it.

There is nothing natural about the processes of human expression and human understanding. Each of us has to learn how to do it.

The important point to remember is that *nothing* we encounter in the world—including words and images—contains or conveys meanings. It is we humans who provide that in every instance. What something means is not what that *something* means, but what it means to the person making the interpretation of some aspect of the world. This includes our most common form of encoding—in words.

Words do not contain or convey meaning. To the contrary, humans impose meanings on words. It is this problematic that Eliot referred to. It is a problem for any attempt to express—in any medium of expression.

The problem exists in a mirror-like way on both sides of the **encoding**-**decoding** divide. Those who want to express something meaningful have to chose the medium and the words or images for doing so. They will then be at the mercy of those who will be the audience doing the decoding.

Photographs may be the most representative of their subjects. But we also have to learn how to *read* photographs. They are not pictures of reality. They represent someone's interpretation and subsequent encoding. The photographer is the encoder. He or she *creates* what we will be presented with. To be meaningful to a specific person or set of persons, even photographs have to be decoded.

So the first prerequisite is that the encoder has to decide what meaning he hopes to elicit in the viewer. Then he has to have the skills that enable him to translate what he imagines onto the finished photograph. All the rest is up to the viewer, the audience, the people doing the decoding.

They have to look upon something that is fundamentally meaningless until it is translated by them into the meanings *they* impose upon it.

This is true for the photograph. This is true for the novel or the poem or the television show. This is true for every utterance in any medium. This is true of apprehending the world. This is as true for news broadcasts as it is for comedy routines or television drama. In choosing an automobile or an outfit, the person doing so is encoding—in hopes that those who apprehend him or her will decode him or her as hoped.

Nothing is meaningful—including a word—until it is decoded: translated, interpreted, disambiguated by some decoder. And that decoder will do so not as commanded by the word, but according to the mind he or she has for doing so.

This may seem overkill. But most people in our culture assume that the meaning is IN what they apprehend. In making that assumption, they create endless problems for themselves. Modern pop psyc and its interpreters say that people are "determined"—by their genes, by past events, by others. This is empirically not so. We *people* determine what things mean—in the context of our subcultures and our larger culture.

Historically and cross-culturally, people have tried many ways of avoiding that reality, including gods and popular psychology. Those can be made to work in the right circumstances.

But, then, *anything* can be made to work in the human world of encoding-decoding, in the virtual world we create and then inhabit by how we do so. We create that virtual world by how we explain things. Then that virtual world creates us.

Intending . . .

Words can take on whatever meaning we acceptably attribute to them.

Thus, *meaning* has come to have another meaning in practice. "Meaning" can be a stand-in for "intention"—as in "I didn't mean to," or "That's not what I meant."

It is a way of "intending" to avoid responsibility for how others decode what we said or did. Rightly so. But how others decode what was said or done is not the encoder's responsibility in the first place. How accurately it represents his or her *meaning* is certainly the encoder's responsibility.

Anything can be misinterpreted—if judged from the viewpoint of the encoder's intentions.

That's the great divide—between the encoder's intentions and the decoder's interpretations. Those who apprehend and those who express have differing agendas. It's a game, always won by the decoders. But that is the challenge—sometimes the intolerable wrestling challenge—referred to above by Eliot.

There is an old English proverb which suggests that:

> "The road to Hell is paved with good intentions."

But then supposedly so is the road to Heaven.

The experienced hell comes from the situation in which the decoder's intentions do not match or sync with the encoders' intentions. When the decoder struggles to get at the encoder's meanings by asking of himself or the encoder, this is the opposite of hell. It is that extremely rare occurrence when communication is perfect. It is what happens when two people "fall in love" with one another. But it takes both—as with all communication: one to utter it, another to believe it.

Behind every communication encounter is a relationship. If all parties have the same intentions regarding the outcome, the *worst* efforts will work. When not, then the *best* efforts may not work.

There are three other matters relating to intending . . . that will reward our attention:

1. **One** is implicit in what Chaucer wrote back in 1395:

   > " . . . *intent is all* . . . . "

suggesting that one may harbor good intentions, or bad. When someone is disambiguating what was expressed, it makes a great deal of difference whether that person assumes good . . . or bad intentions on the part of the one offering the expression. People interpret quite differently given their assumption about the originator's intent.

So you have to know. Or you have to guess. Pickpockets read their victims' intentions. Victims are usually not very good at reading the pickpocket's intentions.

Direct marketers are assumed not to be in business to improve the lives of people, but to improve their cash flow. So if a direct marketer comes along with good intentions, we may throw his flyer into the trash with the others.

Intentions matter.

2. A **second** is touched upon by Shakespeare, when he wrote in *Romeo and Juliet* (c. 1595-96):

    "*. . . my interests are savage-wild . . . .*"

His point is that you cannot actually *see* the intentions of others. You can only guess at them. Then it all depends upon what your own intentions are. If they are win-win, you will guess one way. If they are win-lose, you will guess in quite a different way.

Intentions matter. But they are most often invisible.

If you are not sure of your own intentions, you will increase the ambiguity of the encounter. If the other person is not sure of his, the encounter will be even more ambiguous.

Many of our everyday problems—personally and collectively—stem from the lack of clarity about our intentions. Yet, if you make your intentions known, but the others keep theirs hidden, you are at a disadvantage.

There is no resolution. It's a condition of human communication.

3. The **third** is offered up by the poet and philosopher William Blake, when he wrote (in 1805):

    "*A truth that's told with bad intent*
    Beats all the lies you can invent."

In other words, it is never a matter of simply telling the truth—or not. If you intend to hurt someone, tell them the truth. We lie to avoid doing hurt, when that is not our intention. A doctor or a priest may lie, in order not to exacerbate a person's problems.

Their intention is not to lie. Their intention is to avoid doing harm unnecessarily.

Intentions matter. But the truth of things is not at stake. Lovers lie—in their dress or comportment—in order to get what they want. Their intention is not to lie. It is to accomplish what they imagine needs accomplishing, under the circumstances.

So intentions are secret but powerful players in the process of disambiguating. As an old proverb has it:

> *"A liar is not believed when he tells the truth."*

What assumption would you make? You could be wrong either way. Is there a way to avoid being wrong? Is there a way to be right? The paradox that comes from stereotyping (which we will revisit in a few pages) is age-old.

There may be two more provocations about intending . . . that would be worth your careful consideration.

The wit Oscar Wilde was presumed to have said:

> *"Good intentions don't exist until they are carried through."*

No intentions exist until they have been revealed in their consequences. And then we would be explaining them after the fact. If your intentions are well-meaning, they must be acted upon immediately. How could I know you love me if you didn't treat me like I think a lover should? No one can know what we intend except by how we behave.

What we do and how we do it eliminates the ambiguity of our intentions.

The other paradoxical provocation is this:

> Garrett Hardin, a biologist, pointed out (in the February 1974 issue of *Fortune*) that any intention carried through remains ambiguous for the simple reason that it may have unintended consequences:

> *"You can never do merely one thing. The law applies to any action that changes something in a complex system. The point is that an action taken to alleviate a problem will trigger several effects, some of which may offset or even negate the one intended."*

Systems of every size are complex—including conversations. You cannot say something and expect it will be understood as you intended. It lands on the complex minds of other people. They will interpret what you say as they intend—and as is necessary for them.

In war, these several effects are sometimes referred to as "collateral damage." In human communication, there will always be collateral damage. There will be residual and accompanying effects you may not have intended. Some may even negate the one you intended.

The now-venerable Cause → Effect formula rarely applies. The "Cause" being your intended meaning, the "Effect" being whatever interpretation is made by others. You do not—can not—control that.

How your intentions turn out depend upon many other factors—and often many other people.

Incompetence

You can trust competent people to say what they mean, and to mean what they say. You cannot trust incompetent people. Even though they are likely to be dogmatic about certain things, they are like leaves blowing in the wind.

You can never solidly disambiguate what incompetent people say, or do. And you can never depend upon them to interpret accurately what you say as you intend.

The more incompetent people are, the less capable they will be—at any given moment—of disambiguating what you say, or do. The more incompetent people are in their roles in life, the more self-centered they will be. They assume that everything is about them. They do not readily grasp an abstraction or an objective. If it isn't about them, they lose interest in collaborating with you.

Incompetent people do not comprehend long-term goals, or the tactics required to get there. You can talk about the need, for example, for teamwork. They will not understand, because that involves interdependence and they can't or don't want to go there.

They do not *like* people who appear to be superior to them in intellect or other capabilities. They do not like authority. They have long-since concluded that their opinions are equal to anyone else's. In fact, they do not see their own beliefs as opinions. They are, to them, facts—reality.

As the British novelist and playwright Sir Anthony Hope Hopkins wrote (in 1894):

> *"Your [incompetence] cramps my conversation."*

It is difficult to carry on a fruitful conversation with an incompetent person. There are too many obstacles standing in the way.

Typically, the more incompetent people are, the more arrogant they will be. They abhor the complex—which is almost everything in the modern world. They prefer clichés. The phrase "you know" originated there. They are often never sure of what they mean by what they say, so they sprinkle their talking with "you knows." If you don't know, the whole process collapses.

Harry Truman once quipped,

> *"It is [incompetence] that causes most mistakes."*

He used the word ignorance. But here I think they suggest roughly the same problem. Ignorance seems more like a permanent trait. Incompetence is fixable.

The twentieth-century Indian philosopher and statesman Sarvepalli Radhakrishnan put it this way:

> *"Hindu and Buddhist thinkers with a singular unanimity make out that* avidya *or ignorance is the source of our anguish . . . ."*

Here too ignorance can be read as incompetence. Problems in relationships, in organizations, and between nations stem largely from the incompetence that created them in the first place. And, as Einstein said, you can't solve a problem with the same mentality with which it was created.

The problem in disambiguating—as it is in communication in general—is that of incompetence.

That needs to be addressed first. If you are competent, your problems will seem to be solvable to you. If you are not, they will seem to be insoluble, requiring an intervention from outside to solve them.

The government in the U.S., just as the number of executives in an organization or the number of helpers in a society, grows at the same pace as the incompetence of its members or of the citizenry.

Learning How to Think

Learning how to avoid ambiguity before expressing oneself, and learning how to disambiguate all the other inevitable ambiguities, requires the ability *to think*.

Humans are not born knowing how to think. It is an acquired set of strategies and tactics, not unlike learning how to play the piano or ride a bicycle. It requires time, effort, and commitment.

People who explain things without the ability to think at least adequately about those things are *toxic* to themselves, to others, and to society. They go about spreading the disease of mental stultification to anyone foolish enough to listen to them.

They simplify by generalizing from an instance. They cannot deal with multiple causes, or multiple effects. They prefer that life be rational, no matter how wrong their rationality may be.

Such people explain things along the lines of the explanations they have randomly encountered. If someone offends them, they paint the whole person black. If a male offends them, they write off the whole of the male gender—as in "I know your type, and you're *all* pigs."

People who can't think suffer from mental fast-food and from stereotyping. Thinkers want the particulars. Non-thinkers want the generalities.

Thomas Edison once quipped,

> *"There is no expedient to which a man will not*
> *go to avoid the labor of thinking."*

There is more than labor involved. There is prowess, which comes from years of learning how.

The humorist and columnist Evan Esar described the non-thinker's dilemma thus:

> *"A few people think, many think they think, and the*
> *rest use clichés so they won't have to think."*

So you can see what you're up against when trying to get others to disambiguate the world. A cliché can't be disambiguated because there is nothing behind it anyway.

Then there is the tight connection between thinking and speaking. Speaking is thinking . . . materialized. The famous writer E. M. Forster once put it this way:

> *"How can I tell what I think till I see what I say."*

What people say is a mirror of their minds. Most of those people would argue that those are two entirely different things. They don't want to be embarrassed by the documentation. Thinking and speaking are two aspects of the same thing.

If you develop your capacity for communicating—and for being-communicated-with—you have covered the thinking part of it.

Disambiguating People

Secretly, this is what most people are doing most of the time.

There are many who cannot disambiguate themselves. So they are largely incompetent when it comes to disambiguating other people.

Others are so full of their own rigid opinions that they start with a serious handicap.

As has long been known, it takes a thinker to detect a thinker. All others are merely imposing their own impoverished mental models on the rest of the human world.

About *evidence*: it helps to remember that people gather evidence based on their own theories (mental models) about things. They would much rather explain things to others than to have others explain things to them. Wisdom is priceless. Talk is cheap.

Most people will choose the easy way.

To fail to discriminate is to fail at valid disambiguating. You can't disambiguate people who can't disambiguate themselves—meaning those people who have no particular competencies at life because they have no particular purpose in life.

Millions have tried it . . . and failed.

8

Telling Stories

*"And what if the making up of stories to explain
things, this story-telling that we think we need
to keep us sane, is actually the thing that makes
us crazy?"*

—John Jerome, in *Stone Work* (1989)

When I was young, and when I had done something I should not have done, my mother—as fine a person as ever lived—would gently interrogate me. She would begin by saying, "Don't story to me now."

Meaning, I still assume, that she didn't want an explanation that I spun out to avoid punishment. She wanted a story that made the wrong-doing my fault, and my fault alone.

That was a bitter pill then. It still is. It seems that most people have developed a way of avoiding responsibility for their wrong-doing, and have surrounded themselves with people who welcome their fictions. So they end up slightly or totally not responsible for their wrong-doing. They have learned how to blame external factors—people or events, past or present—for their unacceptable actions.

It's somewhat like becoming a puppet, a world in which somebody or something else is pulling the strings. We get to be the central character in the scheme of things. But we get to exempt ourselves from how we think, what we do, or what we say, or how we feel.

It isn't exactly "The devil made me do it." But it is a way of finding some scapegoat to take the hit. It is often not our intention to escape the blame for our lack of intention. But a person cannot live in a world of people except by his own complicity in the consequences of his thinking, being, doing, saying, and having.

If we can find a scapegoat for our own flab, for example, we will find one—with the help of the government.

And underlying it all are the contributions of our popular psychology. In their attempt to emulate the so-called sciences, pop psychologists go about their business of finding a *cause* for our every behavior. We are merely the *victims* of these causes—from DNA and our brains to road-rage—the latter caused by what, exactly, the traffic?

Too many traffic jams? What is the enraged driver doing there? There are poor drivers, and there are crazy drivers. There always have been.

Self-control is anathema to pop psychology. So is self-determination. After all, if people took responsibility for their own feelings and doings, there would be no need for pop psychologists. More than ninety-five percent of all of the people who have lived on this earth got along somehow without pop psychology.

Is it possible that pop psychology emerged and grew at the same rate as our cultural indifference toward self-control and self-determination?

We need both of those now—desperately. Without them, we have no way of validly explaining ourselves. We shouldn't have such ready-made scapegoats. We are on the wrong path by hiding our complicity from ourselves.

There Are Stories, and then There Are Stories

It used to be that stories were the best way people had of teaching, and being taught. (We probably still learn more from stories than lectures.)

Now we have stories merely to entertain us, to while away our boredom.

We emerged as humans out of the stories we told. We will continue to evolve out of the stories we are telling. If you want to know what will become of us, attend to our stories. Our self-images and our take on the world come from the stories we consume. They *explain* us.

Stories can be read or comprehended at two levels:

- There is the surface level of plot, themes, and characters.
- Then there are the lessons about human beings and doings that are implicit, below the surface.

Given our lust for special effects in movies and TV, and our distaste for complexity and clearly human concerns, it is obvious that our stories are less about our everyday dilemmas and more about technology and anything that can be made to be highly dramatic. We want escape, not engagement, with what matters most.

But, in all fairness, we began that way. In 1775, the great statesman and political philosopher Edmund Burke wrote:

> *"Young man, there is America—which at this day serves*
> *for little more than to amuse you with stories of savage*
> *men and uncouth manners . . . ."*

If the Revolution had failed, we might be better makers and consumers of stories. We might even have treasured such riches.

People are less and less capable of reading what is implicit in stories. We want the literal—to be dazzled and frightened. In our stories, we have lost our concern for what is to become of us. We prefer being victimized by our stories rather than being engaged in what they tell us about ourselves.

That which is the *source* of what is human about us is receding from our consciousness. We want our thrills *now*. We don't want to be concerned about our future or the future of our progeny. We want to live in a *literal* world—not a metaphorical one that the best stories have always presented us.

We don't want to *think* about things that are difficult to think about—like who we are and what we are becoming. We look to our media and our technologies to do that for us, or at least to shield us from any compelling need to do so.

We want to be entertained by our heroes. But we wouldn't want one in the house.

Here is the famous contemporary writer Joan Didion:

"We tell ourselves stories in order to live."

But people are, it seems, as adaptable as rats. We live and have lived in all sorts of conditions. It is *what* we tell ourselves about ourselves in stories that matters. We will live. But how *ought* we to live? That's the second level of stories, the one we can as a people access less and less.

In *The Casebook of Sherlock Homes* [1927], Sir Arthur Conan Doyle said about one of the cases that this is a

". . . story for which the world is not yet prepared."

We may take that observation to remind us that stories never land on blank slates. The person to whom any story is addressed is the one who interprets it, the one who makes something of it—or not. The story is the one people are able to make of it.

And people are variously capable. Some won't get the story at all. For others, the same story may be life-changing.

We have become a *literal* culture. Thus stories that require thinking are becoming rare. The comedy is brazen and infantile (compared to, say, Shakespeare)). The drama is formulaic and heavy-handed. Even journalistic stories are politicized. We may be going "where no one has gone before." But when "Hal" takes over our lives and our destiny, the computers and the droids may like it (but how would we ever know?)

But living in an impoverished, dehumanized world is not the best of all possible worlds for humans.

The Most Consumed Stories

The stories that most people consume most frequently are of course those that occur in advertising—particularly television advertising. We easily over-consume our "infomercials." We readily consume the stories that are the *filler* for the advertising that comes before, during, and after most television programs.

The typical story in television advertising is this: You have a problem—whether you knew it or not. We are offering the answer to your problem—and you ignore it at your own risk.

What is easily glossed in television advertising is that it has an anonymous source and an anonymous target. All mass communication messages are of the sort: "To whom it may concern."

If you think it concerns *you,* it is a "bingo" for the advertiser, and it relieves you of some funds that may be burdening you. It is made to seem familiar by frequent use of the word "You," and by a paid spokesperson who looks right into the camera. It is made to seem that they are looking at you.

They are not. They don't know you and they don't care. They get paid for pretending that they care. They do not. They are caring about the size of their paychecks.

These attempts to make it seem personal do work, at least better than those that are not expensively crafted to *seem* personal.

These stories are *explaining things.* They are sometimes subtle—sometimes not—explaining who we are and who we ought to be, how we feel and what we should do about it, how we look compared to the models used and what remedies there are, and how to be in step with the rest of the world about what we buy, where we go, and what we do.

What we do primarily is consume. We are a consumer culture. This is unprecedented in all of human history. The commercialization of story-telling removes story-telling from people and places it in the hands of those who intend to make money by their story-telling. They typically have no other motives.

The writer and humorist Steven Leacock observed:

> *"Advertising may be described as the science of arresting the human intelligence long enough to get money from it."*

But if the people who believe that they can *buy* better circumstances for their lives didn't exist, advertising could not exist. Our culture is complicit in this unprecedented way of explaining things.

Those who are television addicts are exposed to an ever-increasing flood of programs about crime stories, "reality" stories (which no viewer ever experienced), game stories (where you can win by luck), and heavily-dramatized news. Even the weather broadcasts are made into high drama.

We like our drama vicariously. We wouldn't want it in our own lives. We would rather be bored and turn on the television or read an e-book.

When our purpose for living shifts from some necessity to some indulgence, our lives are diminished. But there is probably a pill for that as well.

The columnist and quipster Evan Esar put it this way:

> *"When funnier-sounding ailments are invented,*
> *advertised products will cure them."*

The key word here is *invented*. Is it possible that ailments—physical, mental, financial—are invented to fit an existing cure? Does this dance go on for ever and ever? If so, is that good advice for how to live?

If we could see who we are through the lens of the advertiser or script writer or producer, would we be inspired? Do we really want to go where these stories would take us?

If, as Esar says, *"Advertising is a trick to get you to spend money by telling you how much you can save,"* is that the kind of algorithm we would choose to live by?

We become what we think. What are we thinking about when we are absorbed in a television program, or a television commercial—or, for that matter, immersed in a newspaper or a gossip magazine?

Embedded Advice

All stories embed some advice. It may be intended. It may not. But it is there, whether we are aware of it or not.

For example, most *gossip* (men and women both imbibe) consists of stories. When gossip was one of the few social entertainments available, it was the source of social order. Few people realize how gossip *about* them channels their lives and their destinies.

When people engage in gossip, they are usually telling stories about other people who are not present. This would seem to be harmless. But images of people and attitudes toward them are formed in such story-telling. And those become a part of every person's social environment—invisible but effective nonetheless.

About gossip, the didactic Greek poet Hesiod (c 700 B.C.) observed:

> *"Gossip is mischievous . . . easy to raise but grievous*
> *to bear and hard to get rid of. No gossip ever dies*
> *away entirely, if many people voice it: it too is a*
> *kind of divinity."*

What he is suggesting is that a person's reputation amongst others functions like a divinity—like a god over which we have no control, but which in imperceptible ways controls us.

As humans, we have no choice but to live in the virtual realities created when people talk to one another. It is *that* virtual reality which comprises our mental lives. It is like gravity. We may not know exactly what it is or how it works. But it will have powerful effects quite independently of our understanding.

On the satirical side, Evan Esar wrote as follows:

> *"Cars do not run down nearly so many people as*
> *gossips do."*

Satirical? Yes. But a truism? Seemingly so.

Underneath all the good or bad it does, gossip also serves to synchronize minds. People tell one another stories about themselves, about how they did this or that, and about why their stories one-up other people's stories.

Whoever tells the most compelling story in any gathering of people who are eager to hear it . . . gains status. And people of higher status than our own must be followed. It's a way of *being* the Joneses when others are trying merely to keep up with the Joneses.

Stories Synchronize People's Beliefs

In order to function socially, we have to have beliefs—implicit theories, actually—about who we are and how the social environment works. The more our minds work like the minds of others in our tribe, the more we can take for granted, and the less we have to weigh every thought we have or every action we take.

We achieve this undergirding synchrony via the stories we tell and the stories we share.

Paradoxically, we like to think of ourselves as more independent (as thinkers) than we really are. Without others, we wouldn't even have what we call thoughts. Beyond our senses, thinking is more of a social activity than it is a private one.

All of our thinking that we may want to talk to ourselves or others about emanates from the mind. And the mind is constructed in—and maintained in—communication with others. As the English poet Lord Byron wrote,

"The beings of mind are not of clay . . . ."

The mind intervenes going and coming, until there are no beings except of mind. We no longer see the world as it *is*, or a person as she or he is. We see them in and through the images we have of them. And those are constructed in communication with others.

Everything that has ever been uttered in the way of explaining ourselves to ourselves is represented after many reinterpretations in how we explain ourselves today. So our minds seek synchronization whether we like it or not, whether we know it or not.

We are in the story we are in because it is the one we were drawn into by the stories we've consumed and the stories we've told.

We have to be reasonably well synchronized with other minds in order to participate in the social games people play—from love to business to religion and politics.

What speaks to us has to be in the context of the virtual worlds we inhabit. What we speak *of* has to be in the context of the virtual worlds that others inhabit. It is ultimately our minds that communicate with other minds. Or not.

What we do not mind in common we cannot speak of. There is always required a minimum of synchrony.

Convincing Pretense

People are always pretending to be who they think they are.

If their pretense is convincing, they get to play that role. If it is not, they may have to audition for another role.

The roles people play are always consistent with the stories they imagine they are in. When others are imagining a different story, the pretense doesn't work. It is almost always easier for a Democrat to address a Democratic gathering than a Republican gathering, and vice versa.

We can only play a role in a story the other accepts. It is not possible to be a lover unless there is another to play the counterpart role. What legitimates their mutual roles is a minimum understanding of the story they are playing out together.

We live in a world in which we don't know how to *do* peace. We don't know how to prepare for peace. We don't know how to conduct peace. We don't know how it might be possible to have a hero or a heroine of peace.

Spouses spar with each other. That's what they learn how to do. That's what the stories they consume and the stories they are encouraged to tell are mostly about.

We know how to think and feel and do what we do because we understand the story we imagine we are playing out. The story is the driver and the sanctifier. We are who we are because we are playing a role in a story. Change the story and we have to be someone else. Divorce is a good example. So is the loyal customer or voter whose expectations are destroyed.

To play a role in a story, we first have to convince ourselves. Then we have to convince others. We audition by pretending to be someone in a role. The ratification has to come from others.

If our pretense is not convincing, the role we wanted evaporates. So we have to find another story to audition for a role in.

Life is pretense. If it works, it works. If it doesn't, we don't get the role.

A rock band without fans is not a rock band. It is how the role plays out that explains who we are. It takes two—or more—to define who we are. Others have to legitimize our pretenses.

Rumoring

When people don't have any way of knowing for sure what is going on, they revert to making up an explanation. Others pick up on this explanation. Since people are most likely to tell others stories that someone else has told them, rumors spread quickly.

Rumoring is a very common way of *explaining things*. In lieu of any authoritative story, we make up one that may meet the plausibility test. If it does, it becomes a widely-believed story.

People have a ready appetite for rumors. Rumoring is like a sudden brush fire. It starts, it is relatively unstoppable, and then it dies, fading away from anyone's attention.

As stories, rumoring satisfies a human need—to have some explanation, *any* plausible explanation—for whatever seems important to us at the moment.

Today's rumors become tomorrow's beliefs. The more people who imbibe in them, the more certainty they seem to have. They are the given explanation until the next one comes along.

As the humorous quipster Evan Esar once wrote:

> *"There's only one thing as difficult as unscrambling*
> *an egg, and that's unspreading a rumor."*

That can't be done. Like a contagious disease, once you are afflicted and in turn afflict others, rumors will have their way with you.

Cunning people like politicians, advertisers, and journalists will actually start rumors that strike them as being advantageous—*to them.*

Stories are not always what they seem. If they become a part of daily parlance, it doesn't matter whether they are true or false. Beliefs are always based on *some* evidence. For most people, apparently, it makes no difference how valid that evidence is.

Rumoring is a form of everyday entertainment. It keeps boredom at bay. It is not subject to any test. The next rumor supplants the previous one. It greases the wheels of socializing.

Compelling Stories, Repelling Stories

We are compelled by stories that fit our predilections. We are repelled by stories that don't.

We are receptive to stories that confirm what we know—or what we would like to become. We ignore or reject stories that conflict with what we already know, or that don't fit our immediate hopes and dreams.

So the stories that sustain us are the stories that people, in large numbers, sustain. Those with real staying power become fixed beliefs. They become fixtures of the cultural context we happen to inhabit.

In a given culture, we synchronize our minds by the way we *explain things*—by the stories we tell and are told.

We keep the ones that are compatible with who we already are, and reject those that cast us in some other light. We are led by the stories we keep. We will go where they take us.

Competing Stories

The underlying dynamic in all histories derives from the competition engaged in to determine *which* stories are to gain ascendance and which stories are to be forgotten.

The struggle between science and religion is one of those. It is still very much with us. The struggle between differing religious beliefs has spawned conflict and wars since the beginning of time. Marital discord comes from the power struggle as to whose story is to be the hegemonic one, just as the power struggles between and among nations are in basis about whose story is to be the hegemonic one.

We forget that the conflict is about whose story is to win, and whose story is to lose. In mortal combat, the story is more important than life itself.

Yet there is no life itself. There are only the lives we have in the stories we believe in and are playing out.

Ideologies are master stories. They spawn and legitimate the stories that people tell to explain themselves or to explain the world. If you make up a story, it will be consistent with the ideologies by which you live. If you imbibe someone else's stories, they will be consistent with the ideologies of that source. *Popular songs become ideologies for their consumers.*

We now live in a world of freedom of speech—meaning, roughly, that anyone can say anything they feel like saying to anyone else whenever they want to (for example, the so-called "social media").

We live in a culture that moves us in the direction of making anyone's *opinion* equivalent to anyone else's. Opinions generate heat. But they don't generate much light. We demonstrate and shout that all opinions are equal, but mine is more equal than yours. Will it be a world in which the one with the loudest tirade wins?

The new intolerance is that "My story is better than your story." Where will *that* take us?

Here's how Mark Twain captured the competition (in *Pudd'nhead Wilson*, c. 1894):

> "It were not best that we should all think alike; it
> is difference of opinion that makes horse-races."

He intended his comment satirically of course. But it does raise the question: Do we want to live as if in a horse-race?

In an address to the Associated Press in 1916, Woodrow Wilson remarked:

> "You deal in the raw material of opinion, and if my
> convictions have any validity, opinion ultimately
> governs the world."

We all deal in the raw material of opinion. That's why collective opinion competes with collective opinion.

Opinion is omnipotent. Its aim is to persuade or destroy. It seems to take us nowhere except into ever more proliferating opinion. We do it to choose up sides. It may have no purpose other than that. It's the modern world's jujitsu. It's the verbal competition for minds: whose opinion (which is a *story*) will win the most minds?

The Pursuit of "Happiness"

A story that gets repeated by large numbers of people becomes a myth. There is probably no better example than that of *happiness*.

The happiness myth is just under the surface of most stories about people and life.

It's always better in the story than in real life. It's always better in our imaginations than it is in actuality. We fantasize about it. We hope for more than we are equipped to deliver. There are fantasies and then there is real life. Those are two different worlds.

That's what leads to frustrations and disillusionments. Many young people go about looking for the man/woman "of my dreams." The only place they would ever find such a creature would be in their dreams. Dreams are what they are. Real life is what it is.

An interesting example is to be witnessed in the television series *Sex and the City*. Here are four thirty-something women who hang out primarily with each other. They are in a sense "married" to each other. Still, the drama part of it has to do with their search for Mr. Right. It can't happen. It can't happen because they are already domesticated, but with one another.

A similar example from the media is *Friends*. Here, an ensemble of two young women and two young men relate to each other their adventures in looking for Mr. or Ms. Right. It can't happen, because their lives are already inexorably entwined *with each other*. From time to time, this can also be observed in *Seinfeld*. The pals already provide what they are looking for elsewhere.

In much the same way, people look for happiness. They want someone to make them happy. But happiness is not a destination. It is a condition, largely out of anyone's control.

Happiness is most likely to occur in the seeking, not in the securing. Once a dreamed-of destination is secured, the excitement is over. Routines take over. Routines do not usually provide happiness. Happiness is in the *wanting*. It usually evaporates in the *having*.

As the philosopher and mathematician Bertrand Russell observed:

> *"To be without some of the things you want is an*
> *indispensable part of happiness."*

It's what we don't have that we imagine would deliver happiness. Having it is another matter entirely.

And it would be well to ponder what the pessimistic theologian W. R. Inge had to say:

> *"The happiest people seem to be those who have*
> *no particular reason for being happy except that*
> *they are."*

And the novelist, playwright, and poet Don Marquis adds:

> *"Happiness comes fleetingly now and then to those*
> *who have learned how to do without it, and to them*
> *only."*

Happiness is a human concept, much storied. But like many story-told concepts, it exists primarily in story form. Those who can live the story could possibly be struck by happiness. Otherwise, it remains as ephemeral as the Holy Grail.

It is a way of explaining things that exists mainly in the explanation. Most people know how to fantasize. But few know how to actually live their fantasies.

What would *happiness* be to a person who had never heard of it?

9

Naming, Defining, Diagnosing

*". . . and have dominion over the fish of the sea,
and over the fowl of the air, and over every
living thing that moveth upon the earth."*

—The Old Testament

"The named is the mother of all things."

—*The Tao* of Lao-tzu (5th-century B.C.)

*"If I know a song of Africa—I thought—of the
giraffe, and the African new moon lying on her
back, of the plows in the fields, and the sweaty
faces of the coffee-pickers, does Africa know a
song of me?"*

—Izak Dinesen [Karen Blixen], *Out of Africa* (1937)

It seems inescapable to avoid the conclusion that human life—conscious human life—began, grows, and evolves by naming things.

To name a thing is to establish a relationship between you and the thing named.

A name is a sort of definition. To define a thing is to put in place a relationship between you and the thing defined. The name and the definitions become a concept. The name is a keyword way of indexing the definition. A name may be idiosyncratic (a cat may have a given name by its owners), or it can be generic (there is a dictionary definition of "cat"). We know a thing by naming it and by defining it. What two or more people in a culture know is generic.

But it enables those people to create the illusion that they are talking about the same thing.

There are concepts that are more or less similarly shared within a culture. There are concepts that are unique to the individual and the mental machinations that get established and exercised over repeated encounters with an increasingly-familiar world.

So the prerogative to name things (whatever its source) gives a person or a language group *dominion* over the thing named.

What calls for our attention here is that *all* relationships enable. But they also constrain. If the thing named now belongs to us, we belong to it. Relationships of any sort are *systems*. And a system is always a system of interdependencies. In that sense, we always belong *to* what belongs to us. The car or the cat we own is never independent of us. We belong to it as much as it belongs to us.

Mutually-constraining habits and routines emerge and take on a life of their own. The car—or the cat—accommodates to us as we accommodate to it.

This is the fundamental dynamic we want to explore here. The named, as Lao-tzu suggested, is "the mother of all things." The world unfolds according to how we name it. Love blooms according to how we define it by our thoughts and actions. The world belongs to us according to how we belong to the world.

Be-ing

Given our Western mindset, we like to think that who we are is personal and private. We like to believe that who we *are* is something that belongs exclusively to us. We are told—by the media, in popular songs, and by our friends and teachers—that it is something we have dominion over.

We perceive ourselves in our inner images—in our imagination. In this process, we seem to be the creator, the producer, the cinematographer, and the director.

We think of ourselves as OUR selves. But our seemingly endless capacity for self-deception leads us, and often misleads us.

This is what Mark Twain had to say:

> *"We do not deal much in facts when we are contemplating ourselves."*

We probably don't deal much in facts where any of our treasured self-deceits are concerned. We seek out confirmation. We avoid, whenever we can, disconfirmation. And besides, if you were to disconfirm who I *am*, you would of inner necessity be wrong. One is always the fixed point in navigating the social world. Others are merely satellites.

We are always the court of final judgment where matters of our own identity are concerned. We may not have named ourselves (but in increasing numbers, we may have). But we would much like to reserve the right to define ourselves.

Yet we can never do so unilaterally if we are to relate to other people, and they to us. Relationships are matters of mutual influence, or of mutual grief. We cannot BE anything without the endorsement of other people.

The longshoreman-cum-philosopher Eric Hoffer provocatively suggested:

> *"We are what other people say we are: we know ourselves chiefly by hearsay."*

There is always an ongoing struggle of whose concept of oneself is to prevail: one's own or that of others.

Actually, we do not know ourselves chiefly by hearsay—unless you consider what a person says to herself about herself is a form of hearsay. How other people treat you and respond to you is early on the only influence on one's self-perception. But when the person begins talking to herself about who she is or intends to be, the tussle begins.

For some people, how others see them is the most important factor. For others—particularly those who have a clear purpose in life, the balance swings in the direction of self- and not other-appraisal. Some people—probably only a few—are less susceptible to external judgments than they are to their own.

Why is this important? The crux of the matter of defining things is self-definition. Those who rely on others to define them also accept the fashions of the day relative to how things in general are to be defined.

They do not see it as their prerogative to define things in a way that contributes to their own purposes—simply because they have no purpose other than fitting in with others.

How most people define things becomes the truth for all of those people. It is this dynamic that creates cultural beliefs, and fashions in thought, *be-ing*, and doing.

And, how one defines oneself will bear heavily on how that same person defines everything else. All definitions are mutually-binding. Going forward, it is always the *relationship* between how one defines oneself and how one defines all else—this is the driver and navigator.

Another useful perspective on this business we call the self is provided by Nathaniel Hawthorne (in *The House of Seven Gables*, c. 1851):

> *"What other dungeon is so dark as one's own heart!*
> *What jailer so inexorable as one's self!"*

The notion that one's self-concept functions like a prison for each of us is age-old. The more it is constructed along the lines of how others perceive that us, the less of a prison it may seem. But then the prison exists in how others perceive us.

This illuminates the never-ending balancing act: Is who you are going to be constructed by others for their own purposes (whatever those may be)? Or are you going to construct yourself for your own purposes?

LEE THAYER

Either way, it will be your jailer. You can't construct yourself if you are chiefly a victim of how others conceive of you. If you would be who you believe you ought to be, you have to change their conception, not yours.

Then there is the question of self-idolatry, as Walt Whitman gave voice to it (in his *Song of Myself,* c. mid-19th-century):

> *"And nothing, not God, is greater than one's*
> *self is."*

We live in a culture that is saturated with that me-above-everything attitude. Who loses? Everyone. If we don't live in a culture that is good for us, we cannot compensate by faultily assuming that we are ourselves good for us. When a person sees himself as the center of the universe—that is, when a person believes that the world began when he or she was born—then what needs to be nourished goes unnourished.

The American Indian, who survived for 35,000 years or so without our pop psyc worldview or our technologies, believed that one's duty was first to the tribe, the collective. And that was to be dispatched with great competence.

Different ways of explaining things can indeed have significantly different outcomes. To be conscientious means to look upon the world as it ought to be—not as it is. We may believe that freedom is *freedom from* conscience. That leads to a very different way of be-ing, and thus to very different outcomes.

Belonging

However else it might be seen, your self is not yours, but ours. Because it is constructed in communication, it takes at least two—usually a whole culture—to make it what it is. So you will not necessarily be talking to those who are going to make of you what ought to be made of you. You will be talking to people who mainly want you to be in sync—with them.

People have always lived in groups of one sort or another. Groupthink is not a recent human phenomenon. It is the oldest one.

You belong to your body. There's no escaping that.

You belong to who you are: changeable but inescapable, even in its changes.

You belong to your past. You are the product of your past.

You belong to your future. Who you are is a mirror of your past and your future, and they are mirrors of you.

You belong to the language(s) you can use. What you cannot express or comprehend cannot belong to you.

You belong to your mind. Its content and its machinations are who you are.

You belong to what belongs to you.

You belong to those you talk to, and they to you.

You belong to whatever it is you are capable of being mindful of.

You belong to history. It moves on, with you or without you.

*You belong to a world of realities which you have no control over, and which can be accessed **only** as you and your communicants conceive and explain those realities.*

You belong to those who have made you what you are—past, present, and future—in which you have been and are forever complicit.

Things belong to you only as you explain them. You belong to them only as you explain them.

It may be useful to "explain" these ways of belonging.

You belong to your body.

Indeed there is no escaping that. We are a part of it. In how we think about it, it is a part of us. There is no belonging more unavoidable. It is the hand you were dealt—this body of yours. You can decorate it, mutilate it, or remodel it. But you will still be its captive.

You belong to who you are.

No matter that who you are may be changing all the time. You can't escape the way you are constructed. You belong to how you think, how you feel, and how you comport yourself. You belong to your habits, your beliefs, your fantasies, and your hopes and dreams. They are not *yours*. You are *theirs*.

You belong to your past.

Everything that has ever happened in your life, and every variation in how you have explained those happenings, have made you who you are.
You are some indecipherable *accumulation* of the choices you have made in the past—or the choices that somehow got made in spite of you. No matter. One thing leads to another anyway. And here you are.

You belong to your future.

Out of your past and your present, your future evolves. You belong to it because you were complicit in your past and your present. And, in this sense, it *belongs* to you. Who you are mirrors your past and your future, and they mirror you.

You belong to the language(s) you can use.

You may try expressing yourself in words, in numbers, in pictures, in graphs or formulae. What you cannot comprehend, you cannot express. You have always been and always will be a captive of your comprehension and expression capabilities. You belong to what you can express, and what you can comprehend.

You belong to your mind.

It does not belong to you. You belong to it. Whatever it contains and whatever its machinations may therefore be, it is the source and the sink of who you are. The mind you have determines the only life you can have.

You belong to what belongs to you.

Your possessions are your jailers. You can't possess something that does not possess you back. This was what Ralph Waldo Emerson was getting at when he wrote: *"Things are in the saddle,*
                And ride mankind."

Belongings are something you belong to as much as they belong to you. You belong to your illnesses and your feelings as much as they belong to you.

You belong to those you talk to, and they to you.

That's because minds are made, modified, or confirmed in communication. Talk is somewhat like a contagious disease. So are the media. What you acquire infects you. What you say infects others. That's just the way it is. There is no way of consciously living independently.

You belong to whatever you are capable of being mindful of.

What you pay attention to puts you in a relationship with that person, or event, or thing. The economics of the mind is thus a matter of ROA (*Return on Attention*). The more trash you pay attention to, the trashier will be your mind. The more irrelevancies you pay attention to, the more irrelevant you will be—to yourself and to the rest of the world.

You belong to history.

Certainly you belong to your own history. You belong as well to the destiny of the culture and the subcultures you belong to. They are always evolving, with or without your permission or even your awareness.

You belong to a whole universe of realities which you cannot control.

You can access those realities *only* as those others you communicate with conceive of and explain those realities. You don't live in that real world. You live in the *virtual worlds* that have been created by the people who preceded you, and those who monitor you in the present.

You belong to those who have made you what you are.

You are a product of how they have enabled your perceptions, conceptions, and relationships in *those* worlds. You may not have been aware of it, but you were complicit in that process of making you what you are. You are now and always will be complicit in that process.

Things belong to you only as you explain them.

And you belong to them—people, events, the machinations of the social world—only as you explain them. *Explaining things* is the heart and soul of being human. Without it, you cannot emerge as a human being. With it, you will be the human that those explanations make of you.

To all these, let us add one more:

You belong to the audience you imagine when you pose or perform for it.

And to that, one more:

You belong to all of those—people, places, things—you believe you belong to.

You may not have been aware of your complicity in creating all of these ways of belonging. No matter. Your permission was never required.

But your awareness of your complicity in creating or maintaining belonging relationships by how you explain things going forward will matter to how your life turns out.

What Is the Evidence of What?

As humans, we have to decide what to call a thing. We sometimes also have to determine whether or not we have the right diagnosis. Things named and defined do not always appear before us in their dictionary form.

Detectives and physicians have to look for clues. They are looking for the evidence that might support—or rule out—the hypothesis they put up against the evidence.

Everyday life is like that. We often have to guess what someone meant by what she said. We look for evidence that would support one hypothesis or another.

There are always two pieces of this process:

1. There is having a name for what you are looking for; and
2. Then there is the ability to accurately detect the clues that would tell you whether or not you are on the right track.

Love is like that. We may have the feeling that we are "in" love. We arrive at that feeling by expressing it in some way. There is unrequited love, and there is love that is requited. Both people have to belong to roughly the same imaginary state of affairs named love—got from their cultures and their own thus channeled experiences.

You might feel certain about your state. But you can never totally know what the other person's state may be. That will always be hidden to you.

So by playing the game of courting—or whatever the game may be called these days—each tries to fathom the other's state.

This is a prototype of what happens in statesmanship, of salesmanship, of poker, of competitive sports, and of war. We want to know what is going on in the other person's head. We want to know what he or she is going to do if we do X or Y.

It is what we have to guess at that adds life to our lives. It is what we have to imagine—as opposed to what we know—that exercises and develops our minds.

Whether in love or in war we seek a status quo. Once we achieve it, we go somnambulistic. We may complain about uncertainty in our lives. But it is certainty that dulls our spirits.

When you neither know the name of what you are looking for, and therefore the evidences (clues) for it, you are at sea without a paddle. This is the condition more and more people live in.

The more definitions you can hold in your imagination about the world, the more possibilities you have for finding what you are looking for. The better you are at creating or extracting evidence, the more successful your sleuthing will be. Both are required.

If you have not learned that the world that you want to understand is there by interpreted evidence, then your understanding will always be mostly hearsay. Many people want to live better lives. But they have no substantial names for what would exist in *that* world. And they don't know exactly what evidence they should be looking for.

So they are stuck being who they never wanted to be, in a world they never wanted to live in. And that's because they don't want to believe that the world is hypothetical. The best hypothesis always wins.

You can't be any more successful at life than your abilities for figuring out *what are the evidences of what.*

For example, all of the preceding is evidence for *what?*

A Song of Africa . . .

The third epigram with which we opened this chapter on "Naming, Defining, and Diagnosing" was provided by Karen Blixen. To refresh, here's what she wrote:

> *"If I know a song of Africa . . . does Africa know a song of me?"*

This can well serve as a marvelous capstone of all that has engaged us in the preceding pages.

Just because you have a concept of, a feeling for, or know a song that defines (for you) someone, or something, or a place . . . doesn't mean that what you have is reciprocated.

The other perspective is the one of knowing. The way you know a place does not mean that the place will know you. Just because you know someone else in a certain way does not mean that the other person will know you in the same way.

Your knowings are yours and the other's knowings are his. If they happen to be going in roughly the same direction makes much possible. But that does not eliminate the fact that the other is not obligated to see you as you see him or her.

Because Dinesen (Blixen) makes the target of her song of knowing an inanimate country establishes the extended metaphor all that more poignantly. But it is never the case that your feelings about someone or some place have to be reciprocated as you might hope expect.

It's likely that Africa did not know a song of her. Eva Peron pretended that her Argentina knew a song of her. But that all came from her. There was no evidence that her feelings were reciprocated.

The point is that we can never know. We can look for the evidence—the clues—but the determinations are ours. We can never know for sure. We just make the best guess we can. Just because you belong to someone in a particular way doesn't mean that they belong to you in the same way.

Still, that's the illusion that makes the world go 'round.

The early 20th-century satirist H L Mencken took this definitive stand:

> "We are here and it is now: further than that all human
> knowledge is moonshine.

But it is the "moonshine" that makes the world go 'round. If we all knew precisely, and if we all knew precisely the same things in the same ways, there would be no game. As it is, the game hinges on the fact that we cannot know for certain. And what each of us knows is always unknown to each other. We can only guess. It is the uncertainties, the guessing that makes life what it is.

As the turn-of-the-century writer Edith Wharton once suggested,

> We are the authors of our own thoughts and feelings and doings. But
> those who "read" us will do with those what they will.

Say or do what we will. People will make of it what they do. Belonging is a tenuous circumstance. It is always based on imagination, on feelings. We belong in ways we never fathomed. Not to belong in ways we desire is always painful and alienating.

The happiest people are always those who expect nothing in return for their song.

"Objectivity"

We should not leave these observations without considering the red herring of objectivity.

It's hard to know what "objectivity" really means—what it comes down to. If five people witness the same crime, but are called upon to testify separately from the others, we end up with five different accounts. Which one—or where—is the "objective" version?

Economists don't agree. Scientists don't agree. People have different tastes in music and food. Which one is the objective taste? Physicians don't agree. Go to a different physician and you're most likely to get a differing diagnosis.

So where is this objectivity? Judging from the television advertising, every OTC pain medicine is claimed to be the "best." How can that be?

We're humans. That means that any observation has to be interpreted. It is impossible for us to get something directly, except for a blow on the head. The world we live in is a world of human interpretations. So can an objective report be any more than some sort of consensus?

What could it possibly mean to "be objective"? It is a chimerical cultural myth. It keeps us from realizing that what we know is all humanly constructed in how we have to explain things in order to make sense of the world at all.

Nothing comes to us pre-named or pre-defined, except by prior human consensus.

The 20th-century French poet and essayist Andre Breton offered the following metaphor:

> *"Subjectivity and objectivity commit a series of assaults*
> *on each other during a human life out of which the first*
> *one suffers the worse beating."*

We are prisoners of our own subjectivity. The world that goes on outside of any one of us is the objective world. To participate in that world, we have to deny our subjectivity.

To borrow a Biblical metaphor, that makes objectivity the Devil. It is ordained others who speak for God. If some un-credentialed individual does, we lock him up. We cannot make the objective world converge with our subjectivity. It has to be accomplished the other way around.

What's In a Name?

In their song "Eleanor Rigby" (c. 1966), John Lennon and Paul McCartney wrote:

> *"All the lonely people, where do they all belong?"*

Where, indeed? It is possible to be alone and not be lonely. There are far more ways of belonging than to belong to other people. Chattering all day on the cell phone would have to be considered evidence of being lonely in the midst of a cacophony of human voices and sounds. There seems to be a desperate longing to be "connected." But connected to whom? To oneself? Or to others? And if others, which others, and in what way?

And how are we to explain things as we *ought* to be?

We have to *perform* a feeling in order to have it, as we will see in the following chapter. There are no human feelings or human concepts in nature. They are ours, and ours alone.

What would it mean to all of us involved in the human project to fully comprehend that as it *ought to be* comprehended?

10

Expression and Experience

*" . . . only beings who are capable of manifesting
a particular emotion are capable of experiencing
it."*

—Anthony Kenny, in *Action, Emotion,
and Will* (c. 1963)

Experience is always private and inaccessible by others. The only evidence we can have about another person's inner life is how he or she expresses it or performs it.

We like to believe, in our rational and pervasive scientized culture, that we can identify a person's emotional state by looking at some condition past or present that *caused* those feelings or emotional state. If a person says he is sick, we look for what caused the sickness. If a person is happy, we look for what caused her to be happy. If a person is depressed, we assume there must be some more or less objective *cause*.

Science looks for the causes of certain effects. And it looks for the effects of certain causes. This works well in biology or chemistry or physics. But the things scientists study do not talk back to them. People do. And people do not live in the worlds scientists study.

People live in a world of *virtual* reality—the world of the mind, created and maintained in human communication. People are not pool balls. They may be comprised of cells. But they are not cells. They are sentient creatures. They live only marginally in a cause-and-effect world. The world people live in is not reducible to causes-and-effects.

Scientists analyze. People invent. There are no skyscrapers or other such *ideas* in the natural (or the physical) world. People live their conscious lives in and through their concepts and beliefs about things—not in and through those things themselves.

As has often been observed over the millennia, this is the difference that makes the difference. People are not obligated to be as the forces of nature would have them be. By talking to one another, they negate the strictures of any natural world outside of them.

So looking into a world people do not inhabit may be the wrong place to look for what accounts for their inner experiences.

An Interlocking Relationship

All of this points to an interlocking relationship between expression and experience.

If you can't express an inner feeling, you can't have it. You can certainly have it internally. But you can't "have" it in the sense that others now know what's going on with you. It has no *objective* existence unless you can express or perform it. Then it might have an objective existence consistent with how you have expressed or performed it.

Consider *love*. You can't have the experience unless and until you have expressed it in some way Then the experience of love you have will be consistent with how you express it (or perform it). You can't have the experience of driving a nail until you drive a nail. You can't actually have the experience of driving a car until you drive a car. You can't really have the experience of being elated unless you express it in a way that others will accept.

You can certainly have your private and inaccessible feelings about this or that. But you won't know what they mean or even how to handle them until you express them in a way that others will endorse. People can drive themselves crazy by how they deal with their inner experiences, as Freud suggested. But you won't be locked up until you perform yourself in a way that others take to be the conditions for being locked up.

What this implies is that people cannot express or perform their inner emotions in just any old way. They have to do so in a way that others have a prior comprehension of.

When you say, for example, "I don't feel good," others understand you by referring to those times when they "didn't feel good" and how *they* expressed it before others. You can't *be* happy in front of other people who don't themselves know how to express being happy.

The American Indian generally believed happiness to be a duty that any individual owed to the tribe. We consider it more along the lines of an effect caused by some condition in our inner or social lives.

In our culture, we assume that our feelings come upon us more or less by immaculate conception—that they just arise in us for reasons we then seek to explain away. Road rage, for example, is caused by the frustrating antics of other drivers. It is an inner condition we "just can't help" having, justified by the circumstances.

Inner experiences have to be explained or justified to ourselves and others in some way. It never much occurs to us that we wouldn't "have" them if we didn't perform them or express them.

And yet that is always at the heart of the mechanism of feeling, emotions, and inner experiences.

We are seldom aware of why we do what we do until we do it. The *motive* is in the immediate explanation, as is the justification. We do what we do and then explain it, to ourselves and to others. If those others "buy" our explanation, we repeat what we did. It is then, as it were, pre-approved.

In *Sister Carrie* (c. 1900), the writer Theodore Dreiser made this observation:

> *"In your rocking chair by your window shall you
> dream such happiness you may never feel."*

Yet why isn't a dreamt feeling a feeling nonetheless? Is it because we think of it as a state of being that has to be sanctioned by others?

To be real to us, our feelings have to be acknowledged by others. Otherwise, we might just be kidding ourselves with our own secrets.

We are always acting out the part we believe we have in some story we believe we are in. Our role in this story requires certain feelings on our part, and makes possible a range of other feelings. It's okay, for example, to be "afraid of flying." But it's not a feeling a candidate for a commercial pilot's license would want to express in public.

What story do you imagine you're in? Therein lies the justification for expressing—and thus for *having*—certain feelings. Some feelings are disallowed by certain stories. Surgeons are not supposed to become faint at the sight of blood.

Back to the rocking chair: It may be that one has to enact (perform) happiness in order for it to seem real, as opposed to merely dreamt of.

The columnist and quipster Evan Esar once remarked:

> *"A good way to perk up your spirits whenever you're downcast is to think back over the persons you might have married."*

Middle-aged people who express real joy in their marriages are often looked upon as just silly. There is a time and place for affection. The lust that might have brought the couple together is celebrated at the time. We consider it unbecoming of one's parents.

So where do such inner feelings come from? And where do they go when they fade away?

They come from what's permissible and what's expected—by those other people you belong to. They come from auditioning them in public. If you get the part, you get to "have" the feelings. They come   or go—from what's sanctioned and what's taboo.

It may be useful to reconsider:

> *Would anyone fall in love if they had never heard of love?*

Would anyone *understand* anything if understanding it was not an okay thing to do?

How we explain things does make a difference. If, as the social observer Herbert Spencer said, opinion is a function of feelings and not of the intellect, does it make sense to think of feeling as cause and not as effect?

What we cannot express, we cannot be seen as "having." So how important is articulateness to feelings? How important are feelings to life? And which ones should those be? We don't have feelings and then express them. We have them in *how* we express them.

"Diseases such as cancer, tuberculosis, and schizophrenia . . . exist, but as patterns of explanation, not as things in themselves . . . ."

This was how it was put in the book *Evaluation and Explanation in the Biomedical Sciences* by its editors Engelhardt and Spicer (c. 1975).

It seems a bit like opening a Pandora's Box. But they must have had a good reason for saying that, anticipating that we Westerners would bristle at that kind of idea.

I think that what the editors of that book were getting at is that we name something, and then we treat that name. There are programs and policies and all sorts of pharmaceutical and surgical remedies. But they address primarily *the condition as we have explained it.*

A diagnosis is a guess. It's a guess that has as its parameters what has been said and written about the condition by people and by the experts. Diseases (and all sorts of physical and mental problems) exist. But they exist for humans only as humans have named and explained them.

People can get struck down by a disease or malfunction without ever knowing it, while those who know how to perform the symptoms of a disease or dis-ease fill the waiting rooms of physicians and hospitals.

What is treated is what is presented, or what the tests say. (The "tests" **say** nothing, of course. Both the patient and the tests have to be interpreted by some human.) The interpreter does not live in the actual world of the disease. Neither does the patient. The patient describes his or her inner experiences. But describing varies greatly. Patients report what patients report and what they think the diagnostician will understand.

It is in that sense that experts make their claim. All kinds of diseases and dysfunctions exist in the natural world. But we humans do not—cannot—live in that world. We live in the world of what we say about those things.

The natural world—the actual world—is whatever it is. But we have to do whatever we do about it in a world once removed: the world we create in how we talk about it.

This is **NOT** in any way related to our cultural myth about mind over matter—for which there is little if any evidence. The natural world—and this includes our bodies with all of its organs—is in no way obligated to be as we see it or say it is. That physical world, which we can only *explain*, is totally indifferent to what goes on in our (human) minds.

We can manipulate that world. But it can also manipulate us—in all of its multifarious ways. We belong to both worlds. But the one we have to live in is the one we have invented by how we have *explained* it.

One Nobel-prize-winning theoretical physicist warned us as follows (in 1958 and earlier):

> *"Since the measuring device has been constructed by the observer . . . we have to remember that what we observe is not nature in itself but nature exposed to our method of questioning."*

What we talk about when we talk about "reality" or "the facts" is not reality. We observe using our own agreed-upon method of questioning. The names and definitions we construct as observers do not reveal reality. At best, they reveal a reality exposed merely to the names and definitions we impose upon it.

And, as Heisenberg himself says, we have to remember that.

Pliny the Elder (1ˢᵗ-century A.D.), wrote in his *Natural History* :

> *"Man is the only one that knows nothing, that can learn*
> *nothing without being taught. He can neither speak nor*
> *eat, and in short he can do nothing at the prompting of*
> *nature only . . . ."*

We are not taught how to be human—how to think like humans think—by nature. We have to be taught by other people, who bring us into the game forcefully. We may imitate nature. But she will never imitate us. We have to make it all up.

Somewhat later in the same writing, Pliny says,

> *"With man, most of his misfortunes are occasioned*
> *by man."*

Engelhardt and Spicer would argue that even our diseases are man-made. They were not on earth before we got here. We *explained* them and they are now a part of who we are.

They are "real" enough. But what we say about them is not. What we do about them is an intervention in the world of nature, of which we know nothing more than what we say of it.

As Heisenberg might have implied, we fail to remember that at our peril.

Performing Experience

As I noted above, none of this has anything to do with the myth of mind over matter. What we really want to get at to our great advantage is the idea of *mind over mind*.

We have no control over what happens in world—whether that is external or internal. But we do have control over how we interpret those happenings.

It is others who authenticate (or legitimate) our feelings, our emotions, and our thoughts. They do this on the basis of how we express them. If we audition and get the part, we now legitimately *have* what we have expressed. For example, the more successfully (in the eyes of others) you express fear, the more fear you will experience.

That's the paradoxical connection between outward expression and inner experience. If you successfully express being the victim of the world around you, the more victimized you will *feel*.

Or, another example: the more successfully you express love, the more of that feeling you will have. The more jealousy you express, the more feeling of jealousy you will have. The more helplessness you express, the more helpless you will *feel*. And so on through the evolving catalog of human emotions.

> *A fascinating practicality of all this is that you can*
> *actually practice and perfect the inner life you want*
> *to have simply by expressing it successfully.*

You can't control what happens to you, or what people say to you. But you can control your interpretations of what happens to you. And therein lies this unique power you have of *mind over mind*. You may import from the culture the belief that certain happenings *cause* you to feel this way or that. That would be a tacit choice to be simply a victim of how you are *supposed to* feel about what happens or what is said around you.

This is what Eleanor Roosevelt wrote in *This Is My Story* (1937):

> *"No one can make you feel inferior without your consent."*

Or, we might add, make you feel anything at all without your consent. Having the feelings you think you ought to have, given the circumstances, requires your full complicity.

It may be automatic on your part. But to feel distressed is like a fashion: we partake of it because others are partaking of it, if the cause is right.
By consent, the wise lady is referring to our complicity. We have the feeling of being distressed or consternated by expressing it before others.

LEE THAYER

Elsewhere (in *You Learn by Living*—in 1960), she wrote:

"You must do the thing you think you cannot do."

When we think and feel unconsciously, we are merely fitting with the crowd. She is saying, don't do that. Think consciously about what you want the outcome to be—for you. Express that outcome outwardly, and you will experience it inwardly.

Perform the experience you would have, and you will have it.

Road rage helps neither the situation nor the persons involved. So why do drivers perform it? They perform it because it is fashionable—under prescribed circumstances—to do so.

What we fail to see most often is that we cannot affect the world by expressing our feelings about what is going on. But we do—*always*—affect ourselves. It is that paradoxical aspect that is most important.

It is not exactly the case, but it is a reasonable rule of thumb:

*The outward performance of any experience essentially **precedes** the internal experience of "having" that experience. When you put this into practice, you are always in control.*

We are led to believe that the experience precedes the expression of it. Much practiced, they seem to occur simultaneously. But it is the expression that *creates* and gives form to the experience, as we will see below.

Creating Experience

First of all, as humans we have no choice. There are no human feelings in the physical world. There are no human feelings in the natural world—beyond the hard-wired need to cry out if hungry, or cold, or physically distressed.

Over the millennia people chose to *explain* the world they inhabited—both external and internal. What we are taught as residuals of that are things like what causes what, like what justifies what, like what leads to what. People defined not the physical or natural worlds, but how we humans were expected to look at them.

We had to *create* our understandings of ourselves and our world. We didn't come with those understandings. We couldn't have copped them from nature or from the physical world. They weren't there.

The feelings that we have, the experiences it is okay to have, the feelings we are supposed to have: all came from human explanations over the sweep of history.

So on the one hand, we are burdened by the feelings and the experiences we are supposed to have. On the other hand, since those were *created* by people like us in the first place, we have the freedom to *create* variations. We have the prerogative to create those experiences that we believe would lead to a better life and a better world.

The feelings and experiences our culture hands us change little by little over time. But our own are subject to immediate modification. Individually, we can create for ourselves the kinds of feelings and experiences we think we ought to be having, given our ownership of our own destinies.

We can do this by expressing them. What we express—and how we do so—determines who we will become.

That kind of creation does not come cheap. It requires the discipline and the bit of wisdom required to think about such things. And it requires the will and the competence to do something about it.

Most people would unfortunately prefer to deny their own complicity and find justification for being victims of what happens to them. In this culture, they will find far more recipes that justify their being victims than they will for determining their own inner lives.

Whether you intend to or not, you create a life and a destiny by how you explain things.

If you purposely created an inner life (an experienced life) by how you strategically set about explaining yourself and your world in an advantageous rather than a disadvantageous way, you would be unique. But that's what these concepts are all about—how to avoid being one of the troubled folk by following their fashions in expressing themselves.

The Nobel prize-winning British novelist and playwright John Galsworthy once made this observation:

> *"One's eyes are what one is, one's mouth is what one becomes."*

We see the world the way we do because of who we *are*. As we express ourselves—not only by our mouths but the myriad ways we perform ourselves—we become the kind of person who expresses himself in that way. It is thus that *how we express ourselves creates how we will experience ourselves and all the rest of the world.*

William James, the noted early American psychologist, wrote in *The Will to Believe* (c. 1897):

> *"All the higher, more penetrating ideals are revolutionary.*
> *They present themselves far less in the guise of effects*
> *of past experience than in that of probable causes of*
> *future experience."*

James wrote thickly. But what one can make of this is that a person who has a worthy purpose in life is not driven by past experiences, but by the experiences he or she seeks in life. That kind of person actually *creates* the experiences he wants or needs rather than being a passive victim of his past experiences.

In the same book, he wrote more succinctly,

> *"Believe that life is worth living, and your belief will*
> *help create the fact."*

What we have added here is that it is not the belief itself that helps create the fact, but expressing that belief—performing it before others.

As you interpret the world, and as you express yourself in that interpreted world, so shall you *become*.

We create ourselves in the way we perform our experiences. Our experiences inhere in how we perform them. We are the master, not they.

We live our lives by the experiences we have. Create the ones you need, and you will create the life you want.

Experiences Enable Heightened Experiences

There is one more perspective on this that forms this rich concept.

It is that—in an ideal world—the real purpose of human experience is to enable further and richer experiences. In the same kind of sane world, experience is supposed to provoke growth, not stop it. In our culture, the premise seems to be: Once you have the requisite experience, you can stop learning, stop seeking more challenging experiences.

For us, it seems, in all kinds of roles good enough is good enough. We believe that past experience qualifies people for higher roles. We believe that credentials are equivalent to being in the learning mode. They are not. One who has stopped learning is a poor prospect for any job or role.

For example, when people get married, they stop trying, assuming they have achieved their goal. In the same way, when people are hired, they have a short period of accommodation and practicing the banalities of their job, and then they essentially "retire" in place.

There is no job—nor any role—in which one's performance could not be improved upon . . . *forever*. We get no more than marginal competence in almost every role—at work or at home. People often get better at drinking beer with their buddies than they do in their jobs. That's because they practice—and because it is expected.

If people are not improving at life, they will become losers at life. If people are not improving at their jobs or their other roles, they will be getting worse. There is no steady-state. You either grow or you begin to decline.

The person who is not in the learning mode as a way of life—as a set of compelling attitudes and habits—will become obsolete, both to himself and to his fellow travelers. We accept obsolescence. Yet we are wary of excellence.

It's our ways of explaining things that takes all of us off in the wrong direction.

The famous German philosopher and social critic Friedrich Nietzsche offered us this pertinent observation in *Ecce Homo* (1888):

> *"No one can draw more out of things, books included,*
> *than he already knows. A man has no ears for that to*
> *which experience has given him no access."*

It is learning that opens the doors of life, not experiences repeated over and over again. What we don't *learn* from our experiences gives us no access to experience beyond past experiences.

It was the notable British statesman William Pitt who publicly said (in 1741) that he wished

> *",that I may be one of those whose follies may cease with*
> *their youth, and not of that number who are ignorant*
> *in spite of experience."*

What he said of course is that experience offers no guarantee in itself against ignorance. Experience is blind. If the one who bets on his experience is blind (who doesn't know or care where he is going), then this would be one more case of the blind leading the blind.

Some have said (as the Russian novelist Alexander Solzhenitsyn did in his Nobel lecture in 1972) that art and literature can be a substitute for experience. But people can learn from either direct or indirect experience only what they are personally *capable* of learning.

It is learning that enables learning, which is the prerequisite for gaining experience from experience. It isn't the experience we gain from. It is how we explain or interpret that experience—that is, what we *learn* from it.

An Amish proverb would fit well here:

> *"Some people never learn anything because they understand everything too soon."*

These days most people arrive at the early stages of senility somewhere between age six and age thirteen.

We Become What We Perform

As we explain ourselves and the world we thus inhabit, and as we perform ourselves in that world, we *become* what we can *perform*.

Anyone who *chooses* his or her future must perform it today.

Being a lover requires learning how to perform better and better in that role. Being the successful CEO of an organization requires performing that role superbly. Being a worthy person requires performing as a worthy person, as Confucius said and Gracian insisted.

If you don't have the right auditors to propel you in that direction, acquire them. Otherwise you will be stymied in your existing status quo.

11

Choice and Chance

"Explanations place all apparent possibilities into the context of the necessary; stories set all necessities into the context of the possible . . . Explanations settle issues, showing that matters must end as they have . . . Explanation sets the need for further inquiry aside . . . ."

—James Carse, in *Finite and Infinite Games: A Vision of Life as Play and Possibility* (1986)

In our heads, we play the game of choice. In reality, we are playing the game of chance.

Most people give too little weight to chance, and too much weight to choice. That's why life is often frustrating. We like to believe that we can choose to make things happen. In reality, things mostly happen to us.

We can imagine we are playing out our intentions—our choices—that we can control what happens. For the most part, we cannot. What happens in this world and in our lives is in no way obligated to be as we might wish it to be. The world has its logic. We have ours. The logic of our intentions in this world does not rule the logic of happenings.

The self-help and motivational industries would have us believe that we can achieve what we intend, choose, or wish for if we will only believe that we can. They would be wrong of course. There is no amount of money that can buy off reality. We might thwart it in some technological way, perhaps. Or by luck.

Just because you love someone doesn't obligate that person to love you back. Where people are concerned, there is no clear cause—> effect at work. The how-to-make-people-do-what-you-want-them-to-do business is thriving. But it's all about hope. Like the cosmetic industry, they are selling hope in a bottle (or, in this case, hope in a recipe for influencing other people). Moses brought down the Ten Commandments from God. There are still more people who don't practice them than those who do.

There is forever the world as you would have it be. And there is the world as it is. Explain that in any way you wish. But reality will always win. Beating reality makes good business for the experts. But what happens tomorrow or next week is not controlled by the experts. It may not even *be* controlled.

You may choose as you wish. But your choices will not change the world. They *could* be helpful. If what you intend is at all feasible in reality, and if you have the necessary wherewithal and perseverance it bring it off, you could get lucky.

Chance does seem to favor the well-prepared and the ingenious, as even Louis Pasteur suggested. You have to be well-prepared and incorrigibly ingenious if you intend to pursue your own intentions—small or large. But even for those rarities, there are no guarantees.

In the fairy-tale, David beats Goliath. "Rocky" did win. But those were one-off flukes. Such fairy-tales may help us cope with an indifferent world. But if you pretend that the fairy-tale *is* the reality you have to deal with, you will be made to pay for your mistake.

To put a point on it: Ninon de Lenclos (the popular name of the famous courtesan Anne de Lenclos in 17th-century France) made this observation:

> *"A man is given the choice between loving women and understanding them."*

Love is a purely human conceit. It exists only in our imaginations—in our feelings. It has all kinds of tangible consequences. But it has no tangible existence.

It is the real world we try to comprehend—to explain. Loving and understanding are two mutually-exclusive mindsets. Thus, she says, you must choose which mode you are operating in. You can't operate in both at the same time. You may "wish upon a star." But the star doesn't care one way or the other.

Complaints Abound

It seems to be a perennial avocation of humans to complain about the misfortunes of what has (or might be) happening to them.

Such ubiquitous complaining originates in the discrepancy between what they intended and what they got. It is, again, a matter of failing to acknowledge that one's choices do not obligate the world of events or other people to acquiesce to those choices.

Such blatant lack of accommodation on the part of other people and the rest of the world can be frustrating. In the scheme of things in the real world, that is of no consequence.

What is of major consequence is how our complaints affect each other. What is also of major consequence is how policy-makers at all levels attempt to right the wrongs about which people complain. So we end up trying to fix the world to suit people's desires.

Policy-makers try to legislate happiness or equality, for example. But what can be done in the world of intentions has no necessary claim on the world of actual happenings. It isn't money or level of consumptions that induces happiness in people. On balance, rich people are no happier than less affluent people. Powerful people are no happier than people who are less powerful. And equality is in the eye of the beholder.

It was Abraham Lincoln who remarked,

> *"Most people are about as happy as they make up*
> *their minds to be."*

In our culture, we tend to think of happiness (and other positive states of mind) as something we deserve, or as something that other people owe us.

But those might be better thought of as something we *owe* ourselves and others.

The eminent 19th-century physician and human observer Sir William Osler suggested that there were untoward consequences of our incessant complaining:

> *"Things cannot always go your way. Learn to accept in silence the minor aggravations, cultivate the gift of taciturnity and consume your own smoke with an extra draught of hard work, so that those about you may not be annoyed with the dust and soot of your complaints."*

Those about you would be more than merely annoyed. They would likely take your venting as license to practice it themselves. Complaining becomes a cultural pastime. Our forebears generally had it much tougher then we do. But they didn't complain as much as we do. It is fashionable to complain.

When conversation flags, people can always talk about their illnesses, their misfortunes, and their mistreatment by the world. It is fashionable to broadcast to others our complaints. It is taboo to seem superior by airing our good fortune. In this, we emulate the media.

It wouldn't have to be this way. For a few thousand years, the American Indian was brought up to understand that happiness (and other positive states of mind) were part of one's *duty* to the tribe. What they had to do was to be done with consummate competence and carried out "in beauty," as they put it.

That makes for a radically different social/cultural environment—and one consistent with Osler's prescription. We believe that happiness, for example, has to be caused by something that happens to us. It rarely occurs to us that being happy is something we owe to others.

Thinking of it as our duty to others is more proactive than our deficit pop-psyc concept of things would lead us. It also says, again, that how we explain things makes a difference in how we are led to live our lives.

Which Is the Better Teacher: Choice or Chance?

We are wont to believe that our knowledge comes from what we can control. We are culturally given to believe that we learn mainly from the choices we make, and that what befalls us is just a negative aggravation in our lives. That could be.

But we wouldn't have to think of it in that way.

The famous French essayist Montaigne (16th-century) in one line turned that way of thinking upside down:

> *"Our wisdom and deliberation for the most part follow the lead of chance."*

That could be made to mean many things. The best use that we might make of it here is as follows:

- One becomes wise only by following the lead of chance. Wisdom may require imagination in its development. But wisdom is evidenced only in the real world.
- If we deliberate only about human knowledge, we become myopic. We can comprehend the real world only by carefully considering its seemingly "chance" happenings.
- Love happens. Do we enjoy it more by analyzing it or by reveling in it?
- What we refer to as randomness or serendipity in the real world may simply be *its* logic. That may be inconsistent with *our* logic in explaining it. Our logic is arbitrary, developed only in how we explain things. Which of the two logics is likely to survive?
- Those who ride with chance ride the swiftest and most certain.
- Useful wisdom is wisdom that enables us in the real world. The rest is merely intellectual gamesmanship.
- We tend to ignore chance in our deliberations, and are thus surprised and unprepared for it.
- Chance favors only itself.
- It's likely that no matter how clever we may try to be, the real world—the world of chance—will outwit us.

So which is likely to be the better teacher: our choices and their consequences, or chance and its consequences?

The real world of what happens by chance may be the best school that could be attended by those who have claims on it or intentions with respect to it. Great leaders—actually, great and accomplished people in all walks of life—have had to learn this.

What can we learn about *chance*—except that it is a central player in any endeavor we undertake? Virtuosos in every field prepare for chance. If *amateurs* do, it is rarely if at all.

As people grow in competence (IF they do) in every role they are called upon to play, they intuitively prepare for chance happenings. Competence in role is always a *prerequisite* for *preparedness*. Those who do not follow this progression will indeed be trivially or seriously aggravated by the world's happenings.

Unintended Consequences

The military sometimes refers to this as "collateral damage"—the harm done to unsuspecting or innocent people by the well-intended actions taken.

Actions (including words exchanged) only occasionally have the consequences intended. But they will *always* have unintended consequences.

Are people—whether the perpetrator or the victim—obligated to anticipate the unintended consequences of what they do or don't do, say or don't say, how they interpret or don't interpret?

It is those unintended consequences that account for most of what we casually refer to as the events or happenings of the day. There is always collateral damage—or advantage—in the unintended consequences of what one other person—or millions of people—do or say as they unwittingly pursue their own lives. Are they responsible for how this affects those close-in or larger generations down the line?

The ancient Chinese philosophers said Yes, for seven generations out. The American Indian said Yes, for five generations beyond. In our culture, we take the position that what's done is gone. We sort of calculate the consequences for those who matter in the present context. We don't know how to deliberate in a way that takes account of the impact of our actions and our policies years into the future.

We build highways to accommodate present traffic, and maybe next year's. We treat people for their ills—not for the good of the civilization.
Even our loves are transient. If they don't suit us at the moment, we offload them. We believe in obsolescence. We do not see the connection between what we say or do today and its impact on the future of our civilization.

We are "contemporary," in all senses of that word. We are prone to think that the world began the day we were born, and that it ends with our death. Increasingly, we cannot see beyond ourselves.

Even so, there will always be unintended consequences. If we are not responsible for those, then they will become the main ingredient in the randomness of things.

Choosing "Intentions"

People choose their intentions. It may be by default, but that is still a choice of which they are the source.

We all know the ancient adage:

> "The road to hell is paved with good intentions."

This has been variously attributed and variously claimed. So we'll just treat it as proverbial.

What that suggests, most immediately, is that people may have good intentions, but they don't carry them out.

What this in turn suggests is that imagining doing the right thing is easy.

Doing it is what's hard. It has to be carried out in the real world. And that requires some competence and commitment that does not come easily.

So what the proverb suggests is that people go to "hell" mainly by default. *Having* a good intention doesn't count for much. In the real world, it's all about carrying out that good intention. Failing to do so is tantamount to having and carrying out an intention to do wrong.

This may be what the Irish writer and satirist Oscar Wilde had in mind when he tossed off this little gem:

> *"The worst work is always done with the best intentions."*

None of us can speak for Wilde. The great advantage of epigrams such as this is that they can be explored from different angles.

One such angle leads to the insight that the best intentions can result in the worst consequences—and, supposedly, vice versa. The worst intentions can produce good outcomes.

Another is that intentions don't much matter. It is the results or the consequences that matter. Intentions are no more than figments of someone's imagination until they are enacted.

Another is that the Old Testament (of our Christian Bible) says that it is the act for which one is responsible. The New Testament has been interpreted to say that an act or its consequences don't matter if the perpetrator didn't *intend* those outcomes. Our legal system distinguishes between a murder that was intended and a murder that was not intended.

It has been argued both ways, both by theologians and by trial lawyers. Such duplicity waters down the whole concept of responsibility. If people are not responsible for unwanted outcomes, then something other than humans is.

When we place the cause of undesirable consequences outside ourselves, we occlude the idea of *choice*. And when we do that we become the pawns of social forces and happenings outside ourselves.

What isn't by choice is by chance.

Whether in our individual lives or in the life of our civilization, the gradual abandonment of choice puts our fate into the vagaries of chance. If we are suffering from a sense of helplessness, of purposelessness, it has the seeds of its poison in the abandonment of choice in favor of external causes. About those causes, we feel impotent. All we ever had was choice (if you remember the teaching story of the Garden of Eden). We forfeited, thinking it was freedom.

What we didn't realize was the cost of the trade-off. All of our humanity lies in the choices we have made and are making. Imperceptibly turning our legitimate choices over to chance makes of us pawns in the great socially-cosmic game of chess.

Fates are easily and everyday chosen by default.

Prognostication

To guess at the future in a chance-driven world is to prognosticate. To interpret the past in a chance-driven world is equally to prognosticate. The seers tell us what our future will be. The tellers tell us what our past should mean to us about us and about our future. Our comprehension of our past is as much a creative act as is our image of our future. History is a fiction based on beliefs. What our future "holds in store" for us are beliefs made into palatable fictions.

Both are human interpretations. As such, they are subject to all human proclivities and ideologies. We tell the story of our past to make it fit our present concerns. We tell the story of the future in a way that is consistent with our present concerns, beliefs, and expectations.

We prophesy in both directions. Our aim is to make our past explanations consistent with out present predilections. And to make our future explanations consistent with what we are convinced about our present.

The problem with prediction is well put by James Truslow Adams:

"Any astronomer can predict where every star will be at half-past eleven tonight; he can make no such prediction about his young daughter."

A calculation can predict what's going to happen in a relatively orderly, controlled natural world such as cosmology. It has no people in it, which would transform its rationality into irrationality.

Where the actions of people are concerned, and where the consequences of their actions are concerned, prediction becomes prophecy—someone's best guess. If we knew precisely what is going to happen, we could preclude it—a favorite theme in some popular films and television series.

Because we can't predict it, we make up a story about it that may seem plausible—at least to the story-teller and his listeners.

If a boxer could predict what his opponent is going to do, his opponent wouldn't do it. That's what makes it a game. If we knew going in who was going to win the football game or the tennis match, we wouldn't need to go in.

People may occasionally say, "I knew that was going to happen," always after it had happened. The wisest prophets are those who check out the outcome first, in order to appear wise.

We like to think we can predict. That is of course what drives gambling. But we are always pitted against the random results of a wheel in spin, or the throw of the dice, or of others who are betting against us. The stock market is not rational. It's not rational because it is played by people who have different strategies for "winning" and are willing to bet on their schemes.

The world in human action is a different world. It is not rational, and therefore cannot be predicted except in the most general way—which is given to us by the Law of Large Numbers. But the person playing the game of blackjack or of marriage is not a large number.

What isn't totally controlled cannot be accurately predicted. That is the dilemma of the astronomer's daughter's whereabouts at half-past eleven.

Premises

Every statement made—whether about oneself or about the world in which we are embedded—is based on premises. Some premises are more obvious than others.

A premise is like a theory. It can be used to generate many further statements.

A premise is an understanding of something that *justifies* the statement made, at least in the perspective of the person making the statement. Those who "buy" the statement at the same time "buy" the premise on which it is based.

People who share theories about themselves or about the world in which they live don't have to justify the statements they make about themselves or about that world. Those statements are pre-justified. They are pre-justified by the unspoken or *tacit* premises on which the statements are based.

All signs and symbols—whether they are images, trends, numbers, or words—are also based on premises. Certain cloud formations function as premises for the weather prediction that follows. How a woman postures or offers facial expressions are premises for an observer's interpretations.

Like statements, actions cannot stand alone. They either fit some widely-held premises or will be considered unacceptable. There are norms for appropriate conduct and there are taboos for what is not. Having sex in public is generally not acceptable. Those who want to flaunt the norms of acceptable behavior use those norms as a premise for operating outside of them.

Ultimately, a premise is an established way of explaining things. Our lives—individually and collectively—evolve from our premises.

The British satirist Samuel Butler offered an intriguing twist on that in his 1912 *Notebooks*:

> *"Life is the art of drawing sufficient conclusions from insufficient premises."*

All premises are insufficient in the sense that they do not guarantee the consequences of basing a statement, a decision, or an action on them. They are merely a way of explaining things that prevails. Our virtual realities are often bested by the real world—which is never obligated to be the way we say it is.

Statements that do not rest solidly on agreed-upon premises (about definitions, for example) end up being partly to wholly incomprehensible. To illustrate that, this outtake from Bill Clinton's Grand Jury testimony of August 17, 1998 may be telling:

> *"It depends on what the meaning of the word 'is' is. If*
> *the—if he—if 'is' means is and never has been, that is*
> *not—that is one thing. If it means there is none, that was*
> *a completely true statement."*

Once a person wanders away from widely-held premises, such as the meaning of common words or syntax, that person crosses over into incomprehensibility.

Comprehensibility requires adherence to commonly-held premises with respect to language and its uses. Move outside those boundaries, and it begins to sound like gibberish.

Premises are constraining. But they are the source of the meaning of any expression.

It is the orderliness of what is said or otherwise expressed that enables us to make sense of it. Premises take the chance out of any encounter we want to explain to ourselves. Because what we want to explain to ourselves must already have been explained by the premises from which it is derived.

We invent the world with our explanations of it. Then it invents us.

But that's Not "Fair"

In our virtual world, as we teach our children, there is such a thing as fairness. Play "fair," be "fair," etc.

But that is pure explanation on our part. In the natural world, there is no such thing as fairness. In the human world, the person who plays fair is an easy mark for those who want to con him or her. In a boxing ring, the fair contestant would be the one who telegraphs his punches.

Rules, yes. Voluntary fairness, maybe not.

Playing by the rules makes social and military games possible without mayhem. A terrorist is a person who operates by *not* playing by the rules. You may like sharks. But they seem to attack shark-lovers and shark-haters alike. They operate by their own logic, not by the logic of fairness.

But this is a good example of how the virtual worlds of our own making may be critically inconsistent with the real world. The real world will not be operating by the principle of fairness.

These are at best parallel universes. When they are not in sync, we are plagued by chance.

Choice never displaces chance. And chance never displaces choice. This is only *a* way of explaining such things. It could turn out to be a very beneficial way of thinking in both worlds simultaneously.

12

Why We Do What We Do

*"In the fight between you and the world,
back the world."*

— Franz Kafka

And, of course, why we don't do what we don't do.

We do what we do, not even what we believe we *ought* to do. And we don't do what we don't do for many reasons—indifference, fear, incompetence, habit, or ignorance (that is, failing to see clearly what we should do).

In either case, the place to start with *any* explanation is simple, substantial, and pragmatic. It is:

Fundamentally, people do what they do for two reasons:

1. *Because they **can**; and*
2. *Because they **have to**.*

You can see immediately how advantageous it is to start with the simple reality.

1. In the normal course of events, people will not do what they are *incapable* of doing. If it's something a person cannot do, it's highly unlikely that he or she will do it.

For example, if a young person doesn't know *how* to clean his or her room, it's unlikely that they will do it. They may offer other explanations, but those won't reveal the underlying reason.

Or, for example, a person who can't play the piano well enough to meet the assumed expectations of the people gathered most likely will not attempt to do so.

Another example: a spouse who decides the other is not meeting his or her expectations may be attracted to someone who might do a better job of doing so.

There may be other, more subjective and more complex explanations. The point is to start with the most likely *basic* cause in making any explanation.

Then, if you have made certain that the person to be blamed isn't doing what they should be doing, move on to more fanciful explanations. But never skip this first step.

2. In the normal course of events, people do what they have to do. This is often misunderstood. It's not a matter of being *forced* to do this or that. There are better explanations.

For example, the most powerful imperative for people, and the one they are least likely to be aware of, is habit. People are enslaved by their habits. They do what they do out of habit, because they do not make the choices. Their habits do.

Or, for example, some people have very active and potent consciences. They do what their conscience tells them to do.

Another example: People vary greatly in how "other-directed" they are. If they imagine that some important auditor—present or not—would insist that they do this, but not do that, they may try to obey.

Still another example: in any gathering, most people will be acutely aware of appearances. That is, they try to *appear* to others as they wish to appear in their fantasies. They pose, costume themselves, and comport themselves as if they were on camera. For those who have such concerns, those concerns operate as an imperative—a *necessity*.

A final possibility: some people may actually have a purpose in mind. If they are trying to accomplish something of benefit to their purpose, that purpose can function as an imperative—again, as a *necessity*.

3. The primary influence on behavior used to be *tradition*. What was traditionally done will be done. What was *not* traditionally done was an aberration. Traditions functioned like a collective conscience, encouraging certain behavior, making other behavior taboo.

But now the primary influence on behavior is *fashion*. It was always the case that people emulated one another. But today it is more likely that we are regularly more connected to the media than we are to one another. So we get more of the clues about how to think, how to look, how to dress, how to comport oneself, and how to feel from the media than from first-hand contact with other people.

For example, we typically expect to eat three meals a day. Where does that come from? There is nothing like that in nature.

Another example: Since the invention and the widespread use of the camera, people pose as if on camera. They see the fashions for facial expressions, for posturing, and for explaining feelings offered by the various media. Chimpanzees might use a reflection in still water. But they do not use mirrors to prepare themselves for being with other chimps.

Still another example: Our cars look a lot alike. We notice out-of-fashion clothing, room décor, or behavior in public quickly. We want to be thought of as with it. So we watch the evidence carefully and emulate.

The daughter's early-teenage son in *On Golden Pond* referred to kissing as "sucking face." In the movies or on television, it certainly looks like that is what's happening. Fashions change. And we change with them.

Some *diseases* are out of date. Others are current. Is it possible . . . ?

British playwright and philosopher George Bernard Shaw offered this provocative notion:

"Fashions are the only induced epidemics, proving that epidemics can be induced by tradesmen."

Or, one might surmise, epidemics can be induced by people talking to one another. Diets and other fashions are forever changing. So, apparently, are many of the diseases we have.

4. Finally, and in general, it may be well to keep this in mind:

> People are more inclined to do or to **be** in a way that requires no explanation. The acceptability of certain ways of doing or being becomes the **motive** for doing so. For most people, the norms of the day reign.

> If a person can account for any behavior outside the norm, then it is possible for him or her to do so. But for those who can't explain away their misbehavior, it is not likely to occur.

Things have to make sense to other people. If one's behavior or one's comportment doesn't make sense to one's auditors, one has to explain away the deviance. What's possible therefore depends in part on how persuasive he or she can be before, during, or after the fact.

Explaining things remains fundamental to any society, and to the life a person might be capable of inventing within a given culture.

Evan Esar, the satirical columnist, may help to put a point on it:

> "Necessity is the mother of invention, especially the invention of lies."

What is not acceptable to oneself or to others has to be explained. The explanation is unlikely to be the *real* reason. As a practical matter, we live in a house of lies. We build our societies and our relationships with others out of an edifice of lies necessitated by the need to *account to* those others for our private feelings and yearnings. Those, we rarely reveal. We fabricate ourselves in the eyes of others. We create our outer and inner worlds, and then those inner and outer worlds create us.

The implications of all of our *explaining things* are profound.

Telling, cajoling, or trying to "motivate" oneself *or others* to do something or to stop dong something doesn't usually work. What people do or don't do is first a subjective machination. Then it may be a social one. Or, very rarely, it may be on purpose. But unless you are the drill sergeant or Mother Superior, you will have very limited success by rational argument, by threatening, or by trying to "motivate" others.

Parents and teachers would be well served to take this to heart. One's friends may be influential. But that's because they **can** be or because they believe they **have to** be. A boss is not very influential if all he or she uses is rewards or punishments of some sort. The possibility of influence exists in the existing relationship, not in external techniques.

Explaining What Matters

What matters most is always personal and most often immediate.

So we are constantly explaining things to ourselves, and asking others to explain things that are of concern to us. But most of what gets explained these days comes from the media. In the commercials, they tell us what our problems are, and offer solutions that we can buy. In the news, we consume vicariously what concerns other people, and what is being done about it.

In our favorite programs, we get engaged in the lives and times of other people who live far more glamorously than we do. The implicit message is always, "You could be more like those people." Those characters seem far more relevant to the world than we seem to ourselves.

But it's too demanding to emulate truly successful people. We make up our deficiencies by being exuberant and industrious *fans* of our celebrities.

To explain something puts us in a relationship with what is explained. And it puts that something in a relationship with us. Before long, we are burdened far beyond our carrying capacity. We become what we are related to. And those people or things become how we relate to them.

We all have relationships with other people, of course. If we did not, we would have no self-consciousness at all. That emerges in our talk and interchanges with other people.

But it may be that our relationships with the things of the world—including the physical and natural environments in which we live—are most revealing of how we relate to people and to ourselves. We live in the worlds of consciousness which have been created by those who came before us. In the present, we perpetuate those worlds often with our unthinking complicity.

We become who we are in the context of those worlds. We become what is possible and required in those worlds. They are in turn enabled and constrained by the minds that created and perpetuate them. Those relationships are fundamental.

We get where we are by explaining things.

Nineteenth-century British essayist Charles Lamb wrote (c. 1883):

"A poor relation is the most irrelevant thing in nature."

Here we might usefully expand upon that maxim. A poor *relationship* is not just irrelevant. It can be damning. Relate to the wrong people and the prognosis for your future is poor. Creating relationships with the things of the world will take you where those relationships go—not where you may want to go, or where you *should* go.

Since those relationships are determined by how we explain those things, we create our own heavens and hells (as Freud suggested). Just because we can explain things doesn't mean that we will necessarily do so to our own benefit.

The 19th-century philosopher and theologian Kierkegaard suggested that the only knowledge that has an essential relationship to existence is *essential* knowledge. If that is the case, then our world today is flooded with unessential knowledge. We seem to have lots and lots of knowledge about everything except what really matters (in Kierkegaard's view).

Another springboard comes from Oscar Wilde, the playwright and satirist, in his *The Importance of Being Earnest* late in the 19th-century:

> *"Relations are simply a tedious pack of people, who*
> *haven't got the remotest knowledge of how to live,*
> *nor the smallest instinct about when to die."*

You didn't get the thrust of his point if you thought that "relations" are only kinfolk. Here's a translation for our purposes:

> *Relationships are simply a tedious collection of*
> *connections we have with the world, and it with*
> *us. We are the creatures who don't know how to*
> *choose those binding relationships well, nor the*
> *courage to know when to eliminate them from*
> *our thinking apparatus.*

We create our relationships with the things of the world by explaining those things. This binds us to them in terms of the explanation. We do the same with people and with ideas. We are caught like bugs in a spider web.

We assume those relationships are neutral. They are never neutral. They affect us now. They channel our journey through life. They blueprint our destiny.

Physicians are usually trained diagnosticians. But not infrequently, they misdiagnose. That sometimes ends in death. We ordinary people undertake diagnoses every day. We could be wrong. Just because we can diagnose doesn't guarantee that our diagnoses will be correct.

We often talk to others about our illnesses. The more we talk, the less reliable our diagnoses are likely to be.

We talk about success—and failure. We will end up agreeing about past failures. But we fail to learn much from our theories. About someone's apparent success: well, it seems to depend on whether we like the person or not. It also depends on whether we think *we* could do what we say he did to be successful. We are more often wrong than right.

Everyone has theories about this or that. None are reliable. They make for good conversation, but usually not much beyond that.

We like to express our "feelings." And we are sometimes curious about other people's feelings and experiences. Those are always private, inaccessible to any other person. So people can explain their feelings however they wish. All we have to go on are their explanations—what they say and do. Even those we must interpret, so we put our own spin on them after they are spun out to us.

In her 1935 *Silence*, the poet Marianne Moore wrote this line:

> *"The deepest feeling always shows itself in silence . . . ."*

If that is the case, then most people most of the time are doing the opposite. That might suggest that people do not share their deepest feelings, but fill their conversations interminably with trivial game-playing where feelings are concerned. If one's private feeling are deep, they are not revealed, because that's not how the game is played.

As the writer and poet James Merrill put it (c. 1969):

> *"Proust's Law (are you listening?) is . . .*
> *What least thing our self-love longs for most*
> *Others instinctively withhold . . . ."*

One's own interests and concerns always come first. We can't talk seriously about *your* longings. We can only talk about *mine*. But, equally instinctively, one won't reveal those.

So the feelings we are most likely to have are those people talk about most. They are not *mine*. They are not *yours*. They are the ones we create in explaining them to each other. Perversely, *we end up having the feelings that can easily be talked about in our own circles.*

Health and illness derive for our lives in much the same way. We can *have* only what can acceptably be explained to others. We may privately have joyful lives. But we can't talk about that to others who want to know what our problems are so they can tell us what *their* problems are.

This is not to deny that we are biological and psychological creatures who suffer and die of our undeclared ailments. We can declare only what others are ready, willing, and able to contemplate. What is outside of our explanations is essentially unknowable.

What we can't explain essentially doesn't exist for us. [1] (See endnotes)

Experience

We give the term "experience" far, far more credit than it deserves.

For many reasons. For example: past experience, no matter how outstanding, does not predict to future performance.

Past experience is usually remembered or reported favorably.

People do not learn from experience. They can learn only from their *interpretations* of their experiences.

A person who is "experienced" is not necessarily wiser or more capable.

People routinely mistake experience for competence. A competent person never *arrives*. He critiques his experience in order to become more competent.

A person who has lots of experience uses it as an excuse to sit back and bask in his or her experiences.

Experience should never be taken as a basis for selecting someone. It's what that person is going to contribute to an organization's or a relationship's future that matters.

A person who *wears* his or her experience like a crown will ultimately be a loser.

People who are busy pushing their past usually don't have much in mind for the future.

A person who is in the *learning mode* will in due time outperform those who are not.

In any role, it isn't experience that matters. It is present and future performance that matters.

For all of these reasons and more, the concept of experience is greatly overrated. Anyone who explains himself to others in terms of his experience could simply be lying. A person who explains himself in terms of how he is going to perform and what he is going to contribute in the future nay also be lying. But there is always a *reality check* on that.

The English poet Samuel Taylor Coleridge made this observation:

> *"To most [people], experience is like the stern lights of*
> *a ship which illumine only the track it has passed."*

What's wanted is a track record *going forward*. Explain that, and expect that. Especially expect that of yourself.

Relevance

We create relationships in our explanations of the things, the ideas, or the people or events that interest us. Those relationships exist for us essentially in how we explain those things. We become relevant to them in our explanations of them. They are relevant to us in our explanations of them. We believe in our explanations.

What is not relevant to us we typically don't notice. Heroes are people whose cause is more relevant to them than any pain or exhaustion they might otherwise attend to. People who are trying to accomplish something see the world differently than those who aren't. Those who do not have a purpose focus on their discomforts and victimization. Those who do have a purpose focus on what they are trying to accomplish. They are not deterred by petty concerns.

> *For some, it is the future that is most relevant. The present*
> *is their springboard, not a set of impediments.*

For others, it is the past that is most relevant. They see the
present in terms of their past. Their future is someone
else's problem, not theirs.

We live in what we believe to be relevant to us. If nothing much is relevant to us, we live there. If we see ourselves as relevant mainly to our aims in life, we live for those aims.

The differences for the lives we live are so extreme as to be discontinuous. A rich life does not come from more irrelevance. It comes from the outlook that only *dedication* to cause or purpose produces—that is, only from what is relevant because that is what makes us relevant.

We can understand things only in terms of their meanings—to us individually and collectively. What we can't understand is irrelevant to us. Unless, of course, we fall in love with the person or the thing we can't understand.

The satiric columnist Evan Esar once wrote:

"Poets and babies are wonderful creatures, mainly
because no one can understand what they say."

That's clever. But it's not quite right. Mothers often seem to be able to understand what their babies are "saying." And there *are* people who understand poets. Usually they are either poets themselves, or because they have fallen in love with a particular poet—or with poetry in general. If you don't understand love, you can't "have" it.

We *are* what things mean to us. We attend to ourselves and to all the rest of the world according to what we—and all the rest of the relevant world—means to us. We pay attention to what is relevant to us. And what is relevant to us is given in what it means—to us.

Is a stomach ache distressful if we are unaware of it? Relevance is the key.

We are made of meanings. Meanings are who we *are*. We are relevant to the world in terms of what that world means to us.

And we *can* understand poets who offer us meanings that push our boundaries. We can if we're willing to have our boundaries pushed. For example, the poet T. S. Eliot wrote (in his *Four Quartets*, c. 1941):

> "Music heard so deeply
> That it is not heard at all, but you are the music
> While the music lasts."

The more unconscious you are of the meanings you attribute, the deeper they are. When the process is so deeply ingrained in us, we are not aware of it. So what something means to us is a function of how relevant it is to who we have become.

We ARE the meanings, while the meaning lasts. What you mean to me affects what I mean to you. And vice versa.

What something means to you largely determines what you can mean to it.

Endnotes:

[1] The crux of the matter is this:

> *We live in three worlds—the private world of our own thoughts and feelings, the world of the cultures we inhabit and the people relevant to us, and the world of nature, both internal and external.*

> *All other people have to go on is how we perform ourselves. How others see us ultimately determines who we become. So we are always a product of how others interpret us and how we might choose to be interpreted. And that depends not upon our wishes, but upon how compellingly we perform that role.*

> *For others to acknowledge our pain or joy, we have to perform it convincingly. We have to offer up the symptoms that others can "read."*

*We can make of ourselves only what others will permit
or endorse. If we cannot convincingly perform the role
we want, we can't have it.*

Reality will have its way with us regardless.

That's roughly why we do what we do and why we don't do what we should.

13

Afterword

It's always too late for "the truth."

Our explanations either precede our saying and doing, or they coincide with our saying and doing. That's why it is always too late for the truth.

In either case, we make up our explanations. We are self-fabulists. We deceive ourselves and others in our explanations of things. If there is a truth, it will have its way—with no concern at all for our explanations of things.

With our traditions, our conventions, our rituals and our routines, we keep the truth at bay.

So it is always too late for "the truth."

ABOUT THE AUTHOR

For more than sixty years, the author has been intensely involved in learning how to think widely and deeply about the subjects he examines in this book—and about how these potent ideas can be applied to redirect our own lives and the destiny of our civilization.

Explaining Things, along with his prior *Communication!,* are the culminating fruits of those wide and deep scholarly adventures.

He has taught in several of this country's top universities, and has served as Distinguished Visiting Professor in major universities from Canada to Mexico, and from Finland to Australia.

He was one of the founders of communication as a field of study. He first developed and then edited the journal *Communication* for more than ten years, and has been a sought-after contributor to several of the leading academic journals.

Dr. Thayer was broadly educated in the humanities, in engineering, and in the social sciences, and has an authoritative voice both in the U.S. and around the world.

He is a trained therapist. As a humanist and a renaissance man himself, Thayer is a consummate teacher.

The author is the leading exponent of the role of communication in the human condition, and in human and social evolution in general. He draws upon the wisdom of the world's best thinkers in his work.

In these two books, and in the two volumes that follow, the author establishes a truly multidisciplinary genre that is without peer for every reader who is keen to think more incisively about the fundamentals of all human and social life.

Edwards Brothers Malloy
Thorofare, NJ USA
June 26, 2012